Labourer in the Vineyard

A Portrait of
Pope Benedict XVI

GREG WATTS

LION

A Lion Book
an imprint of
Lion Hudson plc
Mayfield House, 256 Banbury Road,
Oxford OX2 7DH, England
www.lionhudson.com
ISBN 0 7459 5218 6

First edition 2005
10 9 8 7 6 5 4 3 2 1 0

A catalogue record for this book is available
from the British Library

Typeset in 9.5/12 Palatino

Printed and bound in Great Britain
by Cox & Wyman Ltd, Reading

Labourer in the Vineyard

To Suha, who, I hope, will always remember my phone call from St Peter's Square on Tuesday 19 April 2005, to tell her about the 'good man' whose name had just been announced.

Succisa Virescit
(ever pruned, it grows again)

the motto and coat of arms of the
Monastery of Monte Cassino,
the mother house of the
Benedictine order, in Italy

Contents

Introduction

Subiaco

Clinging to the side of a mountain where two valleys meet, the Monastery of St Scholastica, with its twelfth-century bell tower and ancient cloisters, lies near the town of Subiaco, about an hour's drive from Rome. It was here that, over 1,500 years ago, Benedict of Nursia gathered a group of men around him and set in motion a movement that would see hundreds of monasteries – spiritual reservoirs – spring up across the length and breadth of Europe, helping to transform its culture from pagan to Christian. This was largely achieved through men and women following his Rule, a practical guide for daily life.

On Friday 1 April 2005, with the world's attention focused on a window in the papal apartments, behind which Pope John Paul II lay on his bed, dying, a quietly spoken, unassuming German with snowy-white hair was walking through the cloisters of the monastery to receive the St Benedict Award for the Promotion of Life and the Family in Europe.

After accepting the award with a gentle smile and his customary modesty, he began to address those sitting in front of him. His theme was the dangers facing a Europe that was tearing up those Christian roots that Benedict had helped to nurture. God was being excluded from public life, he said, technology was racing ahead of morality, and civilization was threatened by terrorism and the possibility that now existed to manipulate the origin of human life. In a firm voice he continued:

> The rejection of reference to God is not an expression
> of tolerance which wishes to protect non-theist
> religions and the dignity of atheists and agnostics, but
> rather an expression of the desire to see God banished

9

definitively from humanity's public life, and driven into the subjective realm of residual cultures of the past.

That which we need above all in this moment of history are men who, by means of an illumined and lived faith, render God credible in this world. The negative testimony of Christians who spoke of God and lived against him has obscured the image of God and has opened the gate to unbelief.

What the twenty-first century needs, he continued, was men and women who 'hold their gaze directly towards God', who are 'illuminated by the light of God' and who 'open their hearts' to him. Only when men and women allow themselves to be 'touched by God' will the world be changed.

The message would have been listened to particularly closely because it was spoken by Cardinal Joseph Ratzinger, the prefect for the Congregation for the Doctrine of the Faith for the last 24 years and Pope John Paul's top theological adviser.

However, Pope John Paul died the next day, at 9.38 p.m. Rome time, sending the media around the world into a frenzy. What kind of man would now be chosen to lead the Catholic Church?

That night in his apartment in Piazza della Citta Leonina, just outside the Vatican City walls, Cardinal Ratzinger would have recited Compline from his breviary, but he might have spent longer than usual in prayer. For, as dean of the College of Cardinals, he had to guide the Church through a process of transition as it prepared for the conclave to elect the 265th successor of St Peter, the Bishop of Rome. His tasks would include presiding over daily meetings of the College of Cardinals, who would govern the Church in this interval, preaching at Pope John Paul's requiem Mass and then overseeing the conclave that would take place behind the locked doors of the Sistine Chapel.

He had taken part in the two conclaves of 1978, but the majority of the cardinal electors (those under 80) now packing their bags for Rome were having to speedily read up on the complex process and rituals involved in electing a new pope. For the first time the cardinals would now have decent accommodation, in Domus Sanctae Marthae, a modern hotel inside the Vatican. In the past, some of them had been forced to sleep on camp beds in draughty hallways in the Apostolic Palace.

Pope John Paul II

The health of 84-year-old Pope John Paul, who suffered from Parkinson's disease, had been deteriorating. He was admitted to Rome's Gemelli hospital on 1 February 2005, where he had a tracheotomy. Following a second spell in hospital, he was unable to lead the Easter celebrations in St Peter's. However, on Easter Sunday he appeared at the balcony to give his usual *urbi et orbi* blessing to the world, but his words had to be read by an archbishop. He said that he offered his 'sufferings so that God's plan will be realized and his word spread among peoples'. The following week, he died.

Hearing the news, the huge crowd that had kept vigil in St Peter's Square immediately broke into applause for the life of one of the most extraordinary popes in recent times, as the bells of St Peter's solemnly tolled in the background. A Pole and the first non-Italian to hold the office since the Dutch Adrian VI in the sixteenth century, Pope John Paul was a dynamic, charismatic and radical figure on the global stage. Kneeling down to kiss the ground at each of the 129 countries he visited, blessing vast roadside crowds from his white 'popemobile' and celebrating huge Masses became his trademarks. He preached about the redeeming love and forgiveness of Christ, and the urgent need for humanity to return to God. He spoke out in defence of the unborn, the

11

oppressed, and the vulnerable, and championed human rights. He rejected modern Western attitudes to relationships and upheld marriage and traditional Catholic teaching about the place of sex in relationships. And he challenged world leaders to strive for peace, justice, a fairer distribution of the world's resources and an end to poverty. He also sought to heal divisions within Christianity and with other religions.

His death and who might succeed him was a massive story for the media. They didn't come much bigger than this. Journalists from all over the world flew into Rome's Fiumicino Airport, with the Vatican Press Office issuing nearly 6,000 press accreditations. It was to be the first conclave covered by 24-hour TV news channels. Satellite dishes sprouted from the rooftops of the buildings surrounding St Peter's Square and TV crews more used to reporting on the latest antics of some pop star or politician mingled excitedly, if uncertainly, with the ever increasing crowds who were arriving. Suddenly, they had to get to grips with an unfamiliar lexicon: *carmerlengo, apostolic camera, dicastery, novemdiales*. Anyone who hoped Dan Brown's *The Da Vinci Code* might have helped them understand all of this was soon disappointed.

The media arrives

At the time, I was working as a consultant at the Catholic Communications Network (CCN), the press office of the Catholic Bishops' Conference of England and Wales, in Eccleston Square, London. Each day, our small team struggled to keep up with the endless phone calls from Sky News, ITN and the other rolling news TV channels requesting interviewees. And up and down the country radio stations – many I'd never even heard of – made Catholicism their top of the hour story. Unlikely as it sounds, the *News of the World* asked for a 1,000-word tribute to Pope John Paul from Archbishop Peter Smith of Cardiff (they never used it) and even *Yoga Magazine* got in on the act. The communications officers in each of the 26 dioceses had never been so popular with journalists. For once, it seemed cool to be Catholic.

Media speculation about the successor to Pope John Paul had begun well before his death, with talk of the 'runners and riders'. Would the cardinals revert to an Italian? Or would he be a Latin American? Or even an African? Would he be someone who centralized decisions in the curia or someone who gave the local bishops' conferences a greater say? Would he be a liberal or a conservative? What would his attitudes be to issues such as celibacy, artificial contraception or the ordination of women?

The fast-talking American writer John L. Allen Jr. – whose excellent book *Conclave* found its way into many suitcases – helpfully divided the cardinals broadly into two groups, those concerned primarily with the inner life of the Church and those more concerned with the wider world.

With over half of the world's 1.1 billion Catholics now living in the Third World, the constitution of the 115 cardinal electors was the most global ever. 46 came from Western Europe, 12 from Eastern Europe, 13 from North America, 21 from Latin America, 11 from Africa, 10 from Asia and two from Oceania.

Cardinal Dionigi Tettamanzi, Archbishop of Milan, Cardinal Angelo Sodano, Secretary of State, and Cardinal Angelo Scola, Patriarch of Venice were said by many pundits to be among the main Italian contenders. The Jesuit and biblical scholar Cardinal Carlo Martini had, at one time, been tipped for the papacy. But after announcing his retirement as Archbishop of Milan, he had gone to live in Jerusalem, and there were rumours that he had Parkinson's disease.

The non-Italian front-runners identified by many media pundits included Cardinal Claudio Hummes, the Archbishop of Sao Paulo in Brazil; Cardinal Oscar Rodríguez Maradiaga, Archbishop of Tegucicalpa in Honduras; the Nigerian Cardinal

Francis Arinze, prefect of the Congregation for Divine Worship and the Discipline of the Sacraments; Cardinal Christoph Schönborn, Archbishop of Vienna; and Cardinal Ivan Dias, Archbishop of Bombay. Fortunately all these cardinals didn't require any real verbal gymnastics, but who would have fancied speculating on Cardinal Etsou-Nzabi-Bamungwabi of Congo or Cardinal Armand Gaetan Razafindratandra of Madagascar?

And then there was Cardinal Joseph Ratzinger, prefect of the Congregation for the Doctrine of the Faith, often referred to as the 'panzer cardinal' or – to give the impression that he was a kind of doctrinal Arnold Schwarzenegger – 'the enforcer'. It was widely held that he was a blinkered autocrat who delighted in destroying the careers of theologians. What's more, he was said to be anti-women, anti-homosexuals and had contempt for other Christians and religions. In the run up to the conclave the *Sunday Times*, for good measure, ran a headline entitled 'Papal hopeful is a former Hitler youth.'

As the CCN had set up a temporary office in Rome, at the Venerable English College, which has been training priests since the sixteenth century, I was sent out to cover the conclave, due to begin on Monday 9 April. I sensed an air of expectancy as I sat sipping a cappuccino outside one of the many cafés in Borgo Pio. An era had ended for the Church when the body of Pope John Paul II was placed in a crypt near to what is reputed to be the tomb of St Peter. Now, the first papal election for the twenty-first century was soon to begin.

The world waits
Despite all the predictions from the pundits (myself included), the fact was that any of the 115 cardinal electors who would take their seats in the Sistine Chapel, beneath Michelangelo's famous painting of *The Last Judgement*, could

emerge as Peter's successor. The priests and commentators I had spoken to all agreed that the cardinal electors would not reach a decision until Wednesday at the earliest, but more likely Thursday.

Early on a mild Tuesday evening I threaded my way through the crowds along Via della Conciliazione to St Peter's Square after spending the afternoon at Vatican Radio. Arriving at the barrier at the edge of the square, I was surprised to see that the two large TV screens at either side of St Peter's Basilica were showing the chimney of the Sistine Chapel. Wisps of barely discernible smoke blew in the gentle breeze.

'It's white!' shrieked an American woman, jumping up and down.

'It's not. It's black,' corrected someone else.

I couldn't tell. This pantomime no-it-isn't-yes-it-is continued for some time, as the smoke grew thicker. But, to me, it seemed more grey. I checked my watch. It was 5.45 p.m.

Turning around, I found the vice-rector of the English College standing behind me.

'Watch the bell,' he nodded in the direction of the basilica, adding knowledgeably, 'If the smoke's white, it will start to move.'

I did as he suggested, and then suddenly an Australian voice screamed excitedly from somewhere, 'It is white! Ansa have said so.' Ansa was an Italian news agency with a good track record in having its finger on the pulse of the Vatican, but what it knew that everyone else didn't, I couldn't think.

I continued to peer up at the bell, and then all of a sudden it tilted slowly, almost imperceptibly, before releasing its first peal. As I whipped my mobile out to phone my eight-year-old daughter Suha, the crowds were already hurrying excitedly past me into the square.

It was nearly an hour before Chilean Cardinal Jorge Medina Estevez appeared at the balcony (I'm sure I wasn't the only one who, for a split second, thought that he was the new pope), looking pleased. He paused and then announced what everyone was waiting for: *'Habemus Papam!'* A roar went up and then died down just as quickly as heads craned forward in expectation. The atmosphere was electric. Everyone was thinking the same: who would it be? Would be it be an African? Then Cardinal Estevez dramatically proclaimed, *'Josephum... Cardinalem Ratzinger... qui sibi nomen imposuit Benedictus.'* There were gasps. Ratzinger! It couldn't be. A smiling Cardinal Ratzinger, who the week before had celebrated his 78th birthday, then appeared on the balcony.

Speaking above the cacophony of cheers and applause from the square, he said in Italian, 'Dear brothers and sisters, after the great Pope John Paul II, the Cardinals have elected me, a simple and humble labourer in the vineyard of the Lord. The fact that the Lord knows how to work and to act, even with inadequate instruments, comforts me, and above all I entrust myself to your prayers. Let us move forward in the joy of the Risen Lord, confident of his unfailing help. The Lord will help us, and Mother, his Most Holy Mother, will be on our side. Thank you.'

This book is an attempt to provide a portrait of a man whose journey has taken him from a humble house in Bavaria to the majestic St Peter's Basilica in Rome. Such a brief book can only offer glimpses into who he is, what he believes and what have been the key events that have coloured his life and thinking. It is not an attempt to provide a comprehensive account of the turbulent and challenging times he has lived through in Germany and in the Vatican. Nor is it an in-depth exploration of the theological disputes that surfaced during his twenty-four years as prefect of the Congregation for the Doctrine of the Faith. That, I will leave to others. Pope Benedict XVI is important because, like his 264 predecessors, he will not only shape the future of the Catholic Church but also, to some extent, that of the world in which we live.

1 *A Light in the Darkness*

Childhood

'We ask the Lord who gives us strength to carry this symbol so that each German may look with pride at these banners and that they may fly over all of Germany... We ask the Almighty to make us strong in the coming years in faith, in the will for freedom, and in the confidence that one may ban an organization, but never a movement,' implored the preacher, his eyes flashing.

It was August 1927 and the sunshine of the day reflected the optimism of the thousands of mesmerized faces packed into the large park in the Bavarian city of Nuremberg. It seemed as if a saviour had indeed been born. His name was Adolf Hitler.

Had they heard them, Hitler's words would have fallen on deaf ears with Joseph and Maria Ratzinger as they sat fussing around baby Joseph in their modest house in the village of Marktl am Inn, situated on the River Inn in a corner of south-eastern Bavaria, close to the Austrian border. They were good Catholics who believed that life should be lived according to the Word of God, not the word of new ideologies.

Joseph Aloysius had been born on 16 April, a freezing cold day, and baptized four hours later at the small parish church with water that had been blessed earlier that morning at the Easter Vigil. His parents had married seven years before and by the time of his arrival, his mother had already given birth to Georg and Maria. Joseph's father was a policeman, a stern, morally upright man who came from a traditional farming family, while his mother, a cook, radiated warmth.

Unlike other parts of Germany at the Reformation, Bavaria remained loyal to Rome, keeping alive an unbroken tradition of Christianity that stretched back to the English evangelist St Boniface in the eighth century and ultimately to the days of the Roman empire. After the First World War, which brought Germany to its knees, Catholic youth groups and parents' associations sprang up everywhere, and the Catholic Press Association of Bavaria distributed pamphlets, put on films and lectures and helped in the publication of 13 daily newspapers.

But behind this Catholic character there lurked dangerous currents of thought which were intent on tearing out Germany's Christian roots. In his rallies around the country, Hitler was sowing the seeds of a revolution. It would be very different to the one that had overthrown the Tsars and given Stalin's Communists power in Russia, but it would be just as sinister and violent.

The democratic Weimar Republic, established in 1919 after the overthrow of the monarchy, was powerless to halt the rampant inflation and high unemployment that crushed the lives of Germany's citizens. The Ratzingers were not poor, because his father was guaranteed a monthly salary from the police, yet they still had to struggle to make ends meet. Joseph, like his brother and sister, soon learned to find happiness and joy in the simplest of things, something that was to stay with him throughout his life.

Growing in faith

Joseph enjoyed taking hikes with his mother from the nearby riverside town of Tittmöning, where his family had now moved, across the border into Austria. He later recalled:

There was a special feeling of going to 'a foreign country' by just taking a few steps, although in this country they spoke the same language as in ours and, with a few small differences, even the same dialect. In the fields in the fall we looked for wild lettuce, and by the Salzach in the meadows Mother showed us how to find many useful things for our nativity scene, of which we were particularly fond.

In December 1932, the year before Hitler came to power, the family moved again, this time only a short distance, to the farming village of Aschau am Inn, a close-knit community, centred upon the church and school Joseph attended (as well as a brewery, in whose restaurant the men gathered on Sundays). Village life – births and deaths, weddings, illnesses, sowing and harvesting – was closely intertwined with the liturgical life of the Church.

Like many Catholic families at that time, they prayed at meal times, recited the rosary and went to Mass on Sundays. Joseph's life began to be shaped by the rhythm of the liturgical seasons and feast days of the Church, and he was captivated by its rituals and sense of mystery, as he recalled many years later:

During Advent, the liturgy of the angels (Rotate Mass) was celebrated at dawn with great solemnity in the pitch-black church illuminated only with candles. The anticipated joy of Christmas gave the gloomy December days their own particular character. Every year our nativity scene grew by a few figures, and it was always a special joy to go to gather moss, juniper and pine branches with Father. During Lent, on Thursdays, Mount of Olives devotions were held, whose seriousness and sense of trust in God always penetrated deeply into my soul. Then on Holy Saturday evening, the celebration of the resurrection

19

was especially impressive. Throughout Holy Week black curtains had covered the windows of the church so that even during the day the whole space was filled with mysterious darkness. When the pastor sang the words "Christ is risen!" the curtains would suddenly fall and the space would be flooded by radiant light. This was the most impressive portrayal of the Lord's resurrection that I can conceive of.

He developed a fascination with the missal, the book containing the texts of the Mass:

It was a riveting adventure to move by degrees into the mysterious world of the liturgy, which was being enacted before us there on the altar. It was becoming more and more clear to me that here I was encountering a reality that no one had simply thought up, a reality that no official authority or great individual had created. The mysterious fabric of texts and actions had grown from the faith of the Church over the centuries. It bore the whole weight of history within itself, and yet, at the same time, it was much more than the product of human history. Every century had left its mark upon it. The introductory notes informed us about what came from the Early Church, what from the Middle Ages, and what from modern times.

Hitler and the Church

In 1933 Pope Pius XI, who had spent time in Germany as a nuncio (a papal diplomat), negotiated a concordat with Hitler, himself a Catholic. On paper, it appeared to be a victory for the Church. But it wasn't long before the Church and its schools soon became a target for the Nazis. Four years later, in the encyclical, *Mit Brennende Sorge* (To the Bishops of

Germany: on the Church and the German Reich), Pius launched a scathing attack on Nazism. However, the German bishops' conference response to the Nazi ideology was weak, although some individual bishops did take a more courageous stand against this new creed of supremacy and hate that was refashioning the country.

Joseph's father disliked what he saw in the Nazis. They were criminals, as far as he was concerned. While, like many, he did not publicly oppose them, he subscribed to *Der Gerade Weg*, an anti-Nazi newspaper. As a policeman, he was well informed on local matters, and if he thought any priests were in danger of being labelled enemies of the Reich, he would alert them.

Vocation

When Joseph was 10 years old his parents moved to an eighteenth-century Alpine-style farmhouse on the edge of the neighbouring hill town of Traunstein. The house was dilapidated and had no running water (his mother had to make repeated journeys to the well at the bottom of the garden), but the location was glorious. Looking out of his bedroom window in the morning, Joseph would find himself staring wide-eyed in wonder at the peaks of the Hochfellen and Hochgern mountains.

Music, especially that of Mozart, played a major part in Joseph's childhood. Any musical talents he had were completely overshadowed by those of his brother Georg, who was turning out to be a gifted musician. Joseph later wrote that 'Mozart thoroughly penetrated our souls' and that his music contains 'the whole tragedy of human existence'. When German tanks rolled across the border into Austria in 1938, pushing Europe closer to war, it had an unexpected benefit for him. As visitors stayed away from the world-famous Salzburg music festival, his parents were able to buy good tickets at low prices.

21

Since being in primary school, Joseph had felt a strong desire to teach. He discovered that when he learned something, he immediately wanted to share it with someone else. In addition, his desire to be a priest had been growing inside (although he had briefly considered being a painter and decorator), sown in part, it seems, by the impressive image of Cardinal von Faulhaber in his 'imposing purple'. At Easter 1939, six months before Britain declared war on Germany, 12-year-old Joseph joined his brother Georg at St Michael's minor seminary in Traunstein. A bookish and home-loving child, he found the disciplined community life difficult at first, especially the compulsory two hours of sports each day in the large playground, but soon he learned to adapt to his new classmates and the tightly structured seminary day.

War years

Believing that the future of Nazi Germany lay with its children, Hitler had established the Hitler Youth, which had separate sections for boys and girls. The boys were prepared for military service, the girls for motherhood. In 1936, the Hitler Youth became obligatory – teenagers could be forced to join it against the will of their parents – and like his siblings Georg and Maria, Joseph had to reluctantly sign up.

Europe had now entered a war that had spilled over into Africa and the Far East. Having invaded France, Belgium, Luxembourg, Holland, Denmark and Norway, in 1941 Hitler launched an attack on the Soviet Union. Joseph's father told him that the war would not bring triumph for Germany but rather a victory for the forces of evil. But he was unaware of the extent of this evil. Hitler's massacres of the Jews in the ghettos only hinted at the horrors of the concentration camps that later were to shock the world.

In 1943, when US and British planes began bombing German cities around the clock, 16-year-old Joseph and a group of fellow seminarians were called up for military service and assigned to the Flak, an anti-aircraft defence unit in Munich. He was first posted to a Bavarian Motor Works (BMW) factory that produced engines for planes and then to a railway station at Innsbruck. He had a narrow escape when enemy planes attacked one of the batteries where he was positioned, leaving one of his colleagues dead and many more injured. He couldn't wait to return home.

However, his time in Traunstein was short. In September 1944, he was immediately posted to a camp close to where Austria, Czechoslovakia and Hungary met. Here, he found himself in the company of members of the so-called Austrian Legion, fanatics who had served time in prison. One night, a group of them dragged him out of bed and ordered him to join the feared SS. He refused, and when he told them he intended to be a Catholic priest, they both swore and laughed at him.

Two months later, Joseph was relieved to be given back his civilian clothes and ushered onto a train to take him home. As the train didn't stop at Traunstein, he jumped off, overjoyed to be back in the corner of Bavaria he loved so much and freed from a military whose objectives repulsed him. But his joy was short-lived. Even though the war was all but over for Hitler, three weeks later Joseph was summoned to the infantry barracks in Traunstein. Because of an infected finger, which meant he was unable to shoot, he was largely exempt from military duty, although he was still forced to march through the city with his unit, singing war songs.

With the US Army having now having crossed the River Rhine, he made up his mind to head back home, taking a back road to avoid the risk of being shot for desertion. It seemed as if his choice of route had been a good one until he emerged from a railway underpass and froze as he found himself confronted by two German soldiers. What should he do? Was this how he was going to die? Shot for running away from an army he did not want to belong to? The soldiers, however, seeing that he had his arm in a sling, waved him on.

He hadn't been long home when American soldiers came knocking on the door and announced that they were making the house their headquarters. Suspecting that Joseph was a soldier, they arrested him and, along with a large group of other Germans whom had been rounded up, he was marched to a vast prisoner of war camp at Aibling airport, near Ulm. A few weeks later, in June 1945, after being interrogated, he was released. His resolve to be a priest and serve God and the Church was stronger than ever.

Seminary

Just before Christmas that year, Joseph joined his brother Georg at the major seminary at Freising, one of Bavaria's oldest towns and its former ecclesiastical capital, 32 kilometres north of Munich. That he was one of 120 students embarking on six years of study and spiritual formation could be read as a sign that Catholicism was once again beginning to flourish after the dark days of Nazism.

From the moment Joseph took his seat in the classroom for his first lecture, he had very little free time. The daily timetable in seminaries in Europe in the 1940s was ruled by bells and was highly structured. Studies included Latin, which Joseph enjoyed, as he felt it opened up the thinking of the civilizations of the ancient world, New Testament Greek and Old Testament Hebrew. The heart of the seminary was the chapel, where each day the students attended Mass, the Angelus at midday, and sang Lauds, Vespers and Compline from the Liturgy of Hours. They would not only have been expected to spend regular periods in meditation, but also to take responsibility for keeping the corridors and rooms clean and the gardens tidy. The *magnum silencium* was imposed each night. Particular friendships were discouraged and students learned to accept celibacy as one of the demands of the gospel.

The strict rules and regulations were intended to form a student's character, Joseph would have been told. Sleeping conditions were basic. Students were taught not to be concerned with their personal comfort, but rather with their soul. Each one had to save his own soul first if he was to save those of others. The key to holiness was to cultivate a deep life of prayer, which would help them grow into men of equally deep faith. To help them do this, they had the examples of the lives of the saints, and in particular the patron saint of parish priests, St John Vianney, a simple French parish priest who spent up to 16 hours a day in the confessional.

However, the Christian ideas of the soul and faith that were accepted inside the seminary were now being called into question outside. The mid-twentieth century had become a time of urgent debate about what it meant to be a human being and whether the traditional Christian ideas about God were valid any more. If there was a God, why was he silent? If God was good, then how did you explain the presence of evil, such as in Hitler's concentration camps? Wasn't the world just a cosmic accident and human beings simply matter to be extinguished at death? These questions had been asked since the mists of time, but the new trinity of Darwin, Freud and Marx gave them new credence.

As Joseph set out on his intellectual voyage, he grappled with issues such as these in the works of thinkers such as the German existentialist philosophers Martin Heidegger and Friedrich Nietzsche, who famously proclaimed, 'God is dead.' Alongside them, he read the Jewish thinker Martin Buber, whose book *I and Thou*, which proposed a dialogue between the individual and God, had a major impact on Christian and Jewish theology when it first appeared in 1923.

Just as significant an influence on Joseph's life, however, was the seminary rector, Father Michael Hock. Seminary rectors had a reputation for being stern, distant figures, but the kindness and warmth Father Hock displayed to the students earned him the nickname 'the father'. His gentle personality might have had something to do with the fact that he had spent five years in the concentration camp at Dachau.

Theology

After two years of philosophy, Joseph went on to study theology at the Herzogliches Georgianum, a seminary dating back to the fifteenth century and attached to the University of Munich. Because it had been severely bombed, the theological faculty had been temporarily transferred to the former royal hunting lodge at Fürstenried, in a park just south of the city. The conditions might have been cramped and spartan and the meals frugal, but he was at last studying theology, his passion.

If it was philosophy's job to ask the big questions, it was theology's job to try and answer them. This was a period of radical change in theology. New questions were being asked about how God reveals himself, the composition of the Bible, and the nature of the Church. His teachers introduced him to the two major schools of thought in Catholic theology: Augustinian and Thomist.

St Augustine was a brilliant north African thinker who, in the fourth century, had undergone a dramatic conversion to Christianity; St Thomas Aquinas, an equally brilliant thirteenth-century Dominican friar from Italy, who became known as 'the angelic doctor'. Augustine's books included *Confessions* and *The City of God*, while Aquinas left behind the *Summa Theologiae*. It was not just the 800 years that separated them, they had radically different ways of understanding human nature and sin.

Augustine – the pessimist – is noted for his strong emphasis on the corruption of human nature by sin and the absolute necessity of grace for salvation. His principle was, 'Believe in order to understand.' Reflecting on his struggles in life and his long search to know God, he famously wrote, 'Our heart is restless, until it rests in you.'

Aquinas – the optimist – while not denying sin or the need for grace, placed greater emphasis on the goodness of nature, including human nature. He believed that human beings are orientated towards happiness with God, that 'God... wills for the creature that eternal good which is himself'. But sin sometimes gets in the way of this. 'No one can live without delight,' he observed, 'and that is why a man deprived of spiritual joy goes over to fleshly pleasure.' Shortly before his death, he underwent a mystical experience after which he said, 'All I have written is straw beside the things that have been revealed to me.'

Joseph felt drawn more to the ideas of Augustine, which he found reflected the reality of the struggles of faith. He also was becoming familiar with the ideas of St Bonaventure, John Henry Newman and other Church Fathers, as well as contemporary theologians, such as Hans Urs von Balthasar and Henri de Lubac, a French Jesuit, who had combated Nazi attempts to encourage anti-semitism amongst French Catholics. Joseph was coming to see that the Church should not be an end in itself but, through the lives of its members, its sacraments and liturgy, a sign and symbol of God's presence in the world. And, for him, the Church was rooted in the Bible.

A priest

On 29 June 1951, on the Feast of Ss Peter and Paul, along with his brother Georg and 40 other seminarians, he slowly processed up the aisle of the twin-towered, Romanesque cathedral at Freising. With the congregation singing, 'Veni, Creator, Spiritus', he prostrated himself on the floor, his arms outstretched in the form of a cross, symbolizing his submission to God, and he waited for the moment when Cardinal von Faulhaber would place his hands on his head and then pronounce the words of ordination to the priesthood. When the cardinal did this, Joseph couldn't help but notice that a small bird flew from the high altar, chirping happily.

Three weeks later, he began work as a curate at the Church of the Most Precious Blood in the Munich suburbs, a large, busy parish of intellectuals and government staff and shopkeepers and maids. More used to the tranquillity of the library, he found the endless demands on him hard at first. Apart from celebrating Masses, hearing confessions, officiating at baptisms, weddings and funerals, he had to deliver 16 hours of religious instruction at five different levels each week and run a youth programme.

What was to be Father Ratzinger's one and only spell in a parish lasted little over a year, as his local bishop saw that such a bright mind would be more useful teaching in the seminary at Freising. Yet even in such a short length of time Ratzinger learned two valuable lessons. He saw the need people had for a priest and the comfort he could bring them. And he realized that, if their faith was to be nourished and made strong in a rapidly changing society, new models of ministry would have to be developed.

The academic

Having obtained his doctorate in theology from the University of Munich in the summer of 1953 – the title of his thesis was *The People and the House of God in Augustine's Doctrine of the Church* – he began a meteoric rise in German academia. Even a hapless typist who lost pages from an important manuscript and made errors concerning its numbering and references could not hold him back. By 1958 he had become professor of fundamental theology and dogma at Freising and the following year, aged just 31, he was given the chair in fundamental theology in Bonn, the city on the Rhine that had given the world Beethoven. This was a time when the Catholic Church was experiencing a great revival in the study of the Bible, the liturgy and the Church Fathers, something that would have been reflected in Bonn's cluster of theological colleges run by the Dominicans, Redemptorists, the Divine Word Missionaries and the Franciscans.

Students flocked to Father Ratzinger's lectures. He was full of ideas and insights. The Church, he said, had too many laws, many of which have helped to 'leave the century of unbelief in the lurch instead of helping it to redemption'. To make itself relevant in the contemporary world, he argued, it had to 'get out of its armour' and develop a 'new language' and a 'new openness'.

He was thrilled to meet brilliant minds such as Hans Urs von Balthasar and Karl Rahner, two Jesuits who were part of the German school of theology that, along with the French, had come to dominate Catholic thought, and also Paul Hacker, a Lutheran whose gift for languages was so great that Indians came to him to learn Hindi and Sanskrit. The two of them would often sit up late into the night discussing Luther and the Church Fathers over a bottle of red wine. However, his happiness was interrupted by the news that his father had suffered a stroke. Ratzinger returned home immediately and was at his father's bedside when he died two days later.

In 1958 Pope Pius XII died and after four days and 11 ballots Angelo Giuseppe Ronalli, a rotund, jovial 76-year-old from a humble peasant background, appeared on the balcony of St Peter's to give his blessing to the world. He took the name John XXIII. Because of his age, many saw him as little more than a caretaker pope. They couldn't have been more wrong. His reign was indeed short, less than five years, but he was to dramatically change the course of the Catholic Church and, as a consequence, the life of Father Ratzinger.

2 Revolution in Rome

Vatican II

Within three months of his election, Pope John XXIII had surprised everyone by announcing the Second Vatican Council, now more commonly referred to as Vatican II, which was to become the most important event for the Catholic Church in the twentieth century, if not since the Reformation. And Professor Ratzinger was to have a ringside seat.

With its majestic 133-metre-high dome and vast interior, St Peter's Basilica in Rome spoke to the world of a Catholic Church that was an impregnable spiritual fortress. But that was all about to change. The council envisaged by Pope John was one that would give the Church a spring clean. To some, it was to seem that instead it had begun a complete refurbishment.

By the beginning of the 1960s it was clear that the Church and the modern world were drifting further apart. After two world wars, and with the advances in science and technology, many were beginning to feel that the Church did not have the answers to life's questions. And it was a world of an increasingly secular West, a Communist East and an underdeveloped South.

Councils had usually been summoned to address heresy, as at the first one, when fourth-century bishops from across the Roman empire converged in the city of Nicea, in modern day Turkey. Their main purpose was to discuss how to respond to a Libyan priest who was stirring up confusion by telling people that Jesus was not God. After much heated debate, the Council came up with a summary of Christian belief, which became known as the Nicean Creed, and is still recited in churches today.

However, in the twentieth century, the 2,600 bishops who were to shuttle backwards and forwards between their dioceses around the world and Rome for three years had to debate how the Church should respond to the increasingly fragmented and restless modern world. Yes, the Church might be the City of God, as St Augustine had called it 1,500 years earlier, but what kind of city should this be? How should it relate to those outside its walls? Indeed, should it even have walls?

Cardinal Frings of Cologne had been so impressed by the 35-year-old Ratzinger's theological knowledge and ideas that he bought him a ticket to Rome so that the priest could be his *peritus*, or theological adviser. Rubbing shoulders with bishops and theologians from across the globe was exciting for Ratzinger, who had little direct experience of the Church beyond Germany. And on his trips to the coffee shop he might well have stood in the queue behind Karol Wojtyla, an auxiliary bishop of Cracow in Poland, now, like the eastern part of Germany, under Soviet rule. Some years later Ratzinger said, 'This was a very great time of my life, in which I was able to be part of this meeting, not only between bishops and theologians, but also between continents, different cultures, and different schools of thinking and spirituality in the Church.' But Ratzinger experienced a personal tragedy in the middle of the Council: his mother died.

Sitting amongst the cardinals, bishops and theologians in St Peter's Basilica were observers, not just from other Churches but also other religions. Jesus' prayer that 'they all may be one' had not been enough to prevent Christendom splitting between West and East in 1054 and then, 500 years later in Europe, into Catholic and Protestant. This presence of observers at the Council was a visible sign that the Catholic

Church now considered Christian unity and inter-faith dialogue important issues. They listened to debates (as they were mainly in Latin, there must have been some furrowed brows) on everything from the Bible and religious freedom to the media and family life.

As the Council progressed, Ratzinger detected growing unease amongst those who felt it was becoming a kind of parliament, where opinions seemed to matter more than the tradition and teaching of the Church. Even something as fundamental as the Creed seemed to be questioned. The argument was put forward that the Church should be 'the People of God', which implied a more circular model rather than the traditional pyramidical one of the pope at the top, the bishops and clergy in the middle and the laity at the bottom.

One speech by Cardinal Frings had the bishops buzzing. He spoke about the necessity of reforming the Holy Office – better known today as the Congregation for the Doctrine of the Faith. And the person credited with being behind it was none other than Ratzinger. This increased his reputation amongst the hierarchy as a progressive thinker.

The Council closed in December 1965. Pope John XXIII had not lived to see his project through. Shortly before he died of cancer in 1963, he quipped, 'I have launched this big ship – others will have to bring it into port.' The new captain at the wheel was to be Giovanni Battista Montini, who left behind his cathedral in Milan and took the name Paul VI. He was a donnish and sensitive man who, in the words of a former Rome correspondent of *The Times*, 'had the enviable but potentially inconvenient gift of making each visitor feel that he was the person Montini had been waiting all his life to meet.'

Paul VI, like most, had great hopes that the Council would renew Catholic life and help the Church to respond more effectively to the challenges presented by the modern world. *Gaudium et Spes* (Joy and Hope), the last and longest

The Ratzinger family is pictured in 1938. From left to right: brothers Joseph and Georg, mother Maria, sister Maria and father Joseph.

Joseph Ratzinger as a German Air Force assistant in 1943 during World War II.

Celebrating Mass at a mountain site near the Bavarian town of Ruhpolding, Germany, in the summer of 1952.

In the 1980s Cardinal Ratzinger was called upon to head the Vatican's Congregation for the Doctrine of the Faith, becoming the guardian of doctrinal orthodoxy.

Pope John Paul II signs the new Code of Canon Law in 1983, while Cardinal Ratzinger looks on.

Pope John Paul II salutes Cardinals Giovanni Battista Re (left) and Joseph Ratzinger at the Paul VI Hall, 16 October 2003. Cardinals from around the world descended on the Vatican for the biggest gathering of Catholic Church hierarchy in years, celebrating the 25th anniversary of Pope John Paul II's election.

Cardinal Ratzinger blesses the coffin of Pope John Paul II during his funeral mass in St Peter's Square on 8 April 2005. Leaders from more than 100 nations and a multitude of mourners gathered for the funeral of Pope John Paul II, one of the most cherished pontiffs in history.

Pope Benedict XVI greets the Archbishop of Canterbury, Dr. Rowan Williams, during a meeting in the Sala Clementina on 25 April 2005 at the Vatican. The meeting was part of the Pope's efforts to unite with members of other Christian denominations.

The new Pope Benedict XVI appears on the balcony of St Peter's Basilica after being elected the 265th pope of the Catholic Church, on 19 April 2005.

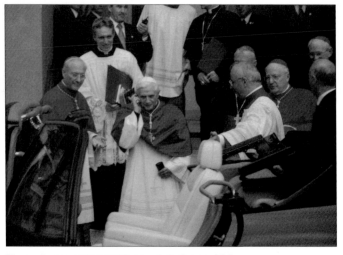

The new Pope preparing for his first tour in the "popemobile".

of Vatican II's 16 documents, began with the words, 'The joy and hope, the grief and anguish of the people of our time, especially of those who are poor or afflicted in any way, are the joy and hope, the grief and anguish, of the followers of Christ as well.'

Civil war

True, the Council Fathers had brought about joy and hope in some Catholics, but also grief and anguish in many others. The most visible and controversial change introduced by the Council was in the Mass, the heart of Catholic life, which had, largely, remained unchanged since the sixteenth century. Mass in Latin had meant that a Catholic could walk into a church anywhere from Buenos Aires to Bombay and know exactly what was happening at the altar (even if they didn't understand all the words).

Now, the priest no longer celebrated Mass in Latin with his back to the people, but instead faced them and used the vernacular language. The congregation now were not spectators but participants. The introduction of communion in the hand and also under both kinds (receiving both bread and wine) emphasized the celebration not just as a mystery and a sacrifice but also a communal meal.

In *The Runaway Church*, Peter Hebblethwaite, who reported on the final session of Vatican II, describes how small groups of Catholics enthusiastically adopted DIY liturgies, replacing bread and wine with rice and tea (to symbolize solidarity with the oppressed people of Vietnam). Priests rejected vestments in favour of boiler suits and readings were taken from Marx and Solzhenitsyn rather than the Bible.

Vatican II had opened up a split in the Church, at least in Europe and North America. The traditionalists wanted to retain the Mass in Latin and devotional practices, such as Benediction, the Rosary and novenas to the Sacred Heart. To them, it seemed as if the Protestants had sneaked in through the sacristy door. One story goes that an ex-Indian army officer campaigned in favour of the Vernacular Society prior to the council and afterwards joined the Latin Mass Society. The progressives believed that new forms of worship were required and that Catholics should leave the ghetto and seek out fellowship with other Christians. Each camp was convinced that their interpretation of Vatican II was the correct one. Documents from Rome warned against improper celebrations, but to little avail, it seemed, and the local bishops fared only slightly better. As one bishop put it, 'A bishop today is like a driver with two passengers – one has his hand on the brake while the other has his foot on the accelerator.'

French Archbishop Marcel Lefebvre had seen enough – he stormed off and set up his own traditionalist seminary in Switzerland, looking back nostalgically to the turn of the century when Pope Pius X pulled up the drawbridge to keep out the enemy, namely those drunk on the liberal spirit of the Enlightenment and French Revolution, and set about turning his attention to Gregorian chant, canon law, the breviary and the seminaries.

These liturgical changes of Vatican II had huge significance for Catholics worldwide. For, as Hebblethwaite points out, 'if change was possible in the sphere of a liturgy which for centuries had remained invariable, then change would be possible in any area of religious life; and that thought led to another which did not long remain unexpressed: where will it all end?'

Ratzinger was deeply unhappy with the new rite, feeling that it had lost the transcendence of the old Mass, and he became alarmed by the way Vatican II had skidded out of control. Mass attendance began to fall, priests and religious resigned, seminary numbers went down, and the authority of priests, bishops and even the pope began to be questioned. As someone who subscribed to St Augustine's pessimistic view of human nature, it was evident to him that much of what came out of the Council derived from those who believed in St Thomas Aquinas' over-optimistic view of the human condition.

Student unrest

Meanwhile, in 1966, Ratzinger left the University of Munster, where he had taught since 1963, for the chair of dogmatic theology at Germany's oldest and most prestigious university, in Tübingen, a picturesque town of cobbled alleys and brightly coloured, half-timbered houses on the sloping banks of the River Neckar, 40 kilometres from Stuttgart.

His appointment was thanks, in part, to a Swiss priest and theologian, Hans Kung. The two men had first met in 1957 at a theological congress in Innsbruck. Kung, like Ratzinger, had been a *peritus* at the council. Although they were both rising stars in Catholic theology, their personalities couldn't have been more different. Ratzinger, a mild-mannered, good listener, who enjoyed playing the piano, Kung, combative, sometimes arrogant and with a liking for sports cars. In his book *The Council, Reform, and Reunion*, he had claimed, 'By far the majority of my demands will find their way into the Council decrees.'

The upheaval in the Catholic Church was a reflection of wider intellectual stirrings in the West. The late 1960s were a time when Marxist ideas about class struggle were beginning to infiltrate universities across Europe, leading to students staging anti-war demonstrations against the US invasion of Vietnam. Paris witnessed the worst street fighting it had seen since its liberation by the Allies in 1944, while Russian tanks rolled into Prague to crush a popular uprising.

Tübingen's theology department became caught up in this new ideological ferment. As dean of the Catholic theology department, Ratzinger found himself on the front line, although most of the trouble he faced was from his colleagues rather than the students. He was determined to counter what he saw as a new spirit in which 'fanatical ideologies made use of the spirit of Christianity'. The Lutheran theology department was under a more serious attack. A flyer distributed by a group of Protestant theology students in the summer of 1969 claimed that the cross of Jesus was no more than an example of glorifying sadomasochistic pain, that the New Testament was a document that deceived the masses and that the Church was an expression of the capitalist system, which exploited the poor. Ratzinger and two Lutheran colleagues formed an alliance to fight back, but they were defeated.

Ratzinger must have spent much time in prayer, perhaps casting his mind back to the promises made by another ideology during his childhood. Before the student unrest broke out he had been working on a book, arising from his lectures at Tübingen, that attempted to explain to a modern audience the message of Christianity. When *Introduction to Christianity* was published in 1968 it received critical acclaim and confirmed him as one of the Church's brightest minds and most effective communicators.

Humane Vitae

If the liturgical civil war ignited by Vatican II was not bad enough, there was a massive explosion in 1968 when Pope Paul VI published the encyclical *Humane Vitae* (Of Human Life). While speaking about the importance of marital sexual love, the encyclical reaffirmed the Church's teaching that only natural contraceptive methods were morally acceptable. If artificial contraception were to become widely available, Pope Paul warned that, amongst other things, marital infidelity would increase and women would be downgraded to sex objects. The Church had to be a 'sign of contradiction', he stressed, anticipating the likely backlash.

In a European society that was experiencing a so-called

sexual revolution, the backlash happened immediately. Many Catholics, including priests, publicly attacked the encyclical. For some it would have been the first time they had openly rejected Church teaching. The French bishops issued a statement leaving birth control to the conscience of individual couples. Cardinal James McIntyre of Los Angeles had to reprimand a mother superior whose opposition to the encyclical landed her on the cover of *Time* magazine.

It was not just for his teaching on birth control that Pope Paul found himself under fire. The year before, he had published *Populorum Progressio* (On the Development of Peoples), whose proposals to bring about peace and justice in the Third World were so radical that they were dismissed by some as 'souped-up Marxism'.

Hans Kung was among those who led the cavalry charge on *Humane Vitae*. Back in the 1950s, Ratzinger had been seen as a progressive and Kung more conservative. But their views had converged by the time of Vatican II when, along with a group of other theologians, they had founded the review *Concilium* in order to provide a platform for new theological perspectives. They had now gone their separate ways for good. For Ratzinger, situations might change, but the substance stayed the same.

Regensburg

Seeking a more peaceful environment, in 1969 Ratzinger packed his books away and left Tübingen for the chair of dogma at the newly created university in Regensburg, a pleasant Bavarian town, dominated by the soaring twin spires of the Cathedral of St Peter, where his brother Georg was choir master. Here, Ratzinger had a small house (with a peaceful garden) built for himself and his sister, who often acted as his secretary.

Ratzinger enjoyed taking groups of students away to a monastery for three-day retreats, where they would discuss theology, pray and in the evenings sit around chatting, laughing and drinking wine and, no doubt, eating Weisswurst, the traditional Bavarian sausage Ratzinger was so fond of. One of his brightest students was Christoph Schönborn, a Dominican who hailed from an Austrian aristocratic family that had produced 19 archbishops, bishops and priests. He was later to become a cardinal.

The following year, Ratzinger teamed up with Hans Urs von Balthasar, Karl Lehmann, Walter Kasper, Henri de Lubac, and leading figures from science, politics and media, to launch a rival publication to *Concilium*, called *Communio*, which appeared first in German and then in Italian. Its aim was to provide an orthodox theological response to what was happening in the Church and culture.

Vatican II's image of 'the People of God' was being taken very seriously in parts of Latin America, where priests, especially Jesuits, were forming 'base communities'. Liberation theology had been born and given shape in *A Theology of Liberation* by Gustavo Guitierrez, a Peruvian priest. The Latin American bishops' conference at Medellin, Colombia, in 1968, supported this attempt to use the gospel to inspire people to build the kingdom of heaven now rather than wait for it in the hereafter. Borrowing insights from Marx, its central idea was that the gospel was not about piety but about liberating people from unjust political, economic or social oppression.

Archbishop of Munich

Ratzinger's reputation was growing in the Vatican, and in 1972 he was appointed to the International Papal Theological Commission. Along with Father Jorge Medina Estevez, a Chilean, who later became head of the Congregation for Divine Worship, and six other members of the Commission, Ratzinger wrote to Pope Paul VI to express alarm that the 'unity and purity of the Catholic faith' was being threatened by inaccurate translations of the liturgical texts from Latin to the vernacular languages. The texts, they argued, should not be left to the local bishops' conferences to judge but rather to Rome.

In July 1976 the Archbishop of Munich and Freising died suddenly and rumours immediately circulated that Ratzinger, who was now dean and vice-president of Regensburg, would succeed him. It was not wild speculation. The year before, at the request of Pope Paul VI, Ratzinger had preached at a retreat inside the Vatican. While the Church, of course, does have those who seek power and prestige, Ratzinger was not one of them. He had no desire to exchange his theology books for the demands of running the Bavarian archdiocese where 75 per cent of its 2.9 million population were Catholic.

When the apostolic nuncio gave him a letter informing him of his appointment as archbishop, he felt unsure what to do. He sought the advice of his spiritual director, who told him, 'You must accept.' Ratzinger went to see the nuncio at the Regensburg hotel where he was staying, then sat down and wrote his letter of acceptance on the hotel's stationery.

On 28 May, 1977, he entered a packed Cathedral of Our Lady, whose distinctive twin towers, topped by cupolas, can be seen far from Munich, and was ordained archbishop. For his episcopal motto, he chose the words 'Co-workers of the truth', from the Third Letter of St John. For him, his faith and his theology had always been about searching for the truth.

Only a month later, he travelled to Rome to receive the cardinal's red hat from Pope Paul VI. Having spent all his life in academia and not knowing many Church leaders in person, he admitted to feeling somewhat overawed by the experience. Only five cardinals were created in that consistory, an unusually low number. In an interview with *30 Days* Ratzinger revealed that he couldn't help but be amused at the consigning of the biretta in the Paul VI Hall:

None of the other four cardinals had a large entourage with him. Benelli had worked for a long time in the Curia and was not very well known in Florence, so there weren't many faithful from the Tuscan city; Tomasek – there was still the Iron Curtain – couldn't have followers; Ciappi was a theologian who had always worked, so to speak, on his island; Gantin is from Benin and it's not easy to get from Africa to Rome. I instead had a great many people: the hall was almost full of people who had come from Munich and Bavaria.

The year of three popes

For the Catholic Church 1978 became known as 'the year of three popes'. In August Pope Paul VI died. Ratzinger, who had developed a great affection for him, was on holiday in Austria when he heard the news. The first thing he did was to phone his vicar general in Munich and tell him to ask the whole diocese to pray for the dead pontiff.

Ratzinger arrived in Rome for the conclave and, after two days, Albino Luciani, the Patriarch of Venice, emerged from the Sistine Chapel as the 263rd successor to St Peter, taking the name John Paul I. Not long afterwards, he sent Ratzinger as his representative to a national Marian congress in the port city of Guayaquil in Ecuador. Ratzinger woke up startled one night to find a shadowy figure at the end of his bed: it was a Carmelite priest informing him that Pope John Paul I was dead, after holding office for just 33 days.

Ratzinger straightaway flew to Rome for an unexpected second conclave. On 16 October, after three days and eight ballots, a beaming Karol Wojtyla appeared at the balcony overlooking St Peter's Square, announced himself to the crowds below as Pope John Paul II and declared, 'Be not afraid. Open wide the doors to Christ.' Aged just 58, he was the youngest pope in over 100 years, the first non-Italian in over 450 years and the first-ever Polish pope.

According to George Weigel (Pope John Paul II's official biographer), soon after his election, the pope wanted to make Ratzinger prefect of the Congregation for Catholic Education. They had first met at the Synod on catechetics in 1977. 'We'll have to have you in Rome,' John Paul said to him. Ratzinger good-humouredly reminded him that he had not long been in Munich, replying courteously, 'you'll have to give me some time.'

On 13 May 1981, Ratzinger, like everyone else, was stunned when the news broke that Pope John Paul had been shot by a would-be assassin in St Peter's Square. Happening at a time when Poland was witnessing a growing opposition from the workers to Communist rule, the attempt had added poignancy. John Paul, however, made a rapid recovery and returned to his ministry with renewed vigour. In November he asked Ratzinger if he would replace the Croatian Cardinal Franjo Seper as prefect of the Congregation for the Doctrine of the Faith. This time he accepted. He must have known that his new post would make him disliked by some of the Church, but he could never have guessed just how much.

3 *Guarding the Truth*

The Vatican

There is a secret religious order that exists behind the heavy walls of the Congregation for the Doctrine of the Faith (CDF), in a large, imposing building on Piazza del San Uffizio, to the left of St Peter's Basilica. These monks, all German and all wearing their distinctive long, pointed hoods, are to be found down in the dark basement. And it is here, in a cold, bare room with a single light bulb, that priests and nuns are brought, sometimes against their will, to undergo long and often painful periods of interrogation about what they believe in.

Cardinal Ratzinger didn't know about these monks when he walked through the doors of the CDF for the first time on a cold January morning in 1982. He didn't know because they don't exist. Many, however, like to think that the CDF resembles this sinister picture.

As he opened his black briefcase in his Vatican office and looked around at the unfamiliar surroundings, Ratzinger must have smiled wryly to himself. For he was now in charge of the same curial department he had – through Cardinal Frings – heavily criticized in that session at Vatican II 18 years earlier.

Ratzinger now moved into a five-storey apartment block above a row of souvenir shops in Piazza della Citta Leonina, just outside the walls of the Vatican City State. The seat of the Holy See, the Vatican, is the smallest sovereign state in the world. Covering just 107 acres, it includes St Peter's Basilica, the largest church in the world, (with the exception of the

Basilica of Our Lady Queen of Peace, in Ivory Coast); St John Lateran, the pope's cathedral, St Mary Major and St Paul's Outside the Wall's; and the Apostolic Palace, where the pope lives. In its attractive gardens are museums, libraries and art galleries packed with priceless treasures.

Apart from this, the Vatican also boasts a post office; a bank; a pharmacy; a 24-hour radio station (set up with the help of Marconi), which broadcasts in more languages than the BBC World Service; secret archives; a prison (just two cells) run by its colourful Swiss Guards; an astronomical observatory and even a railway station. It has its own flag, produces its own stamps and coins, and also a daily newspaper, *L'Osservatore Romano*, which publishes weekly editions in English, French, Portuguese, Spanish and German and a monthly edition in Polish.

The Congregation for the Doctrine of the Faith

The CDF is one of nine congregations in the Roman Curia, which also includes 11 councils and three tribunals. Unlike the councils, which are promotional, and the tribunals, which are judicial, the CDF has executive powers. Founded in 1542 by Pope Paul III, as the Sacred Congregation of the Universal Inquisition, it was given its current name by Pope Paul VI to signal that it was there not to condemn but to promote orthodox beliefs. It was divided into four sections: doctrine, discipline, matrimony and clergy. As prefect, Ratzinger's responsibilities included making sure that the documents and decisions of other departments had no doctrinal implications, handling serious offences involving priests, and meeting with bishops when they made their five-yearly visits to Rome to provide a report on the state of their diocese.

To assist him in his work he had his secretary Belgian Archbishop Jean Jerome Hamer – inevitably nicknamed 'the hammer' by some – as well as a body of cardinals, archbishops, bishops and other expert advisers, along with an administrative team of around 30. His decisions wouldn't be his own. With his new job also came membership of the International Theological Commission and the Pontifical Biblical Commission, each made up of between 20 to 30 professors and providing a link between the Holy See and the theological world, and other Curial departments, such as the Congregation of Bishops and Divine Worship and Discipline of the Sacraments.

Each Friday afternoon, when he left his office and walked the short distance to the Apostolic Palace to meet Pope John Paul in his simple study, he must have pinched himself. What would his father and mother think of him now? Speaking in German, they began with an informal chat, probably even some light-hearted observations about life in the corridors of the Vatican, before moving on to discuss the issues of the day. Ratzinger soon realized that Pope John Paul had little interest in the details of canonical procedures. He was not a details man. It was the big issues – doctrine, catechesis, bio-ethics and social ethics – that really caught his attention. On Tuesdays, the pope would sometimes hold discussion groups, which would begin in the morning and continue over lunch until the middle of the afternoon.

There were those, Ratzinger knew, who saw Church teaching as unnecessarily restrictive in some areas. He didn't agree. In his view, the Church had fixed the borders between truth and error, but, at the same time, along those borders existed space to discover what he called 'new dimensions of faith'.

He knew better than most the battles the Church had been through down the centuries in defence of its teaching. As Christianity took root around the eastern Mediterranean, it had to see off Montanists, Novatianists, Gnostics, Manicheans and others. In 1215, the Fourth Lateran Council called for secular authorities to help the Church combat heresy. Groups of travelling tribunals of Dominicans and

Franciscans rode through Europe to examine those suspected of heresy, and punishment could be severe: Pope Innocent IV condoned the use of torture in some instances.

During his brief spell as Archbishop of Munich Ratzinger had never dodged conflicts, believing that to do so was the worst form of administration. He also believed that dialogue, not accusation, was the best way to try and resolve a problem. This was to remain his approach to the bishops' conferences, superiors of religious orders and theologians he would have to deal with in his new job.

Ratzinger headed up a CDF that was at the heart of a vast network of Catholic dioceses and other ecclesiastical territories containing over 700 million Catholics, or 18 per cent of the world's population. Given this, there would be no shortage of issues – some unpleasant – calling for Ratzinger's attention.

In 1980, Pope John Paul had taken the unusual step of calling a special synod of Dutch bishops in an attempt to hold together a Church moving towards schism as liberals and traditionalists battled over issues such as sexual morality, authority, liturgy, celibacy, and women. In the early 1970s, Ratzinger had been given an account of the Church in the Netherlands after a close colleague made a visit there. Having described the empty seminaries, religious orders with no novices, priests and religious getting up off their knees and quitting, the disappearance of confession, the decline in Mass attendance, his colleague then told Cardinal Ratzinger that, despite all this, Dutch Catholics were optimistic about the future of its Church. However, Ratzinger most definitely was not.

Liberation theology

Ratzinger was clear that one of the most urgent problems confronting the Church was the spread of liberation theology, or, more correctly, theologies of liberation, now trickling out from Latin America and flowing into Asia and Africa. The conference of Latin American bishops that had met in Medillin, Colombia, in 1968 had spoken of 'the preferential option for the poor', structural sin, institutional violence and correct action. But Ratzinger was concerned that the theology underpinning this idea was based more on the concerns of this world rather than the next and that the authentic gospel message of Jesus was getting forgotten. Were those engaged in liberation theology Catholics using Marxism or Marxists using Catholicism? It made no difference. He had made up his mind: this type of theology needed liberating from a secular ideology.

Central America was gripped by fear, violence and murder as revolutionary movements and military dictatorships clashed. As this was the USA's backyard, the CIA was heavily involved. Priests, nuns and lay workers faced daily decisions about how to respond to what they were witnessing. In Nicaragua three priests had become members of the Sandanista government and other priests had taken up arms as part of their struggle for justice. On 24 March 1980, Archbishop Oscar Romero of San Salvador was gunned down while celebrating Mass in his cathedral – because of his defence of the poor and powerless and his vocal criticisms of both left-wing and right-wing extremists. At his funeral, bombs exploded and 20 people were killed and over 200 injured when gunmen opened fire on the vast crowd who had gathered in the square outside the cathedral.

Despite the prominence liberation theology had gained, the majority of priests and bishops in Latin America did not support it. Cardinal Eugenio in Brazil and Cardinal Alfonso Lopes Trujillo in Colombia had warned against its dangers. For Ratzinger, an option for the poor meant that social justice had to go hand in hand with Catholic teaching and beliefs. Yes, the message of Jesus was about liberation: liberation from sin and deception to freedom and truth.

Liberation theology, Ratzinger concluded, did not grow out of grassroots struggles against oppression, as their supporters maintained, but was an imperialistic export from European and North American intellectuals. The kind of liberation theology Ratzinger supported could be found in the life of Mother Teresa, an Albanian nun who had gone to live in the slums of Calcutta and set up the Missionaries of Charity to care for the poor, the sick and the abandoned, or in Cardinal Jaime Sin, who challenged the corrupt regimes in the Philippines. Christians, of course, had a duty to be engaged in the struggle for justice and peace. Pope John Paul had wasted no time in getting behind the rights of the workers living under Communist rule in his native Poland in that momentous first visit there in June 1979. The difference was that the Polish workers stayed within the Church, while liberation theologians ventured beyond it. In an article in the magazine *30 Days*, Ratzinger argued that liberation theology was 'setting up a class struggle inside the Church'.

In 1983 Ratzinger wrote to the Peruvian bishops, asking them to examine the work of Gustavo Guitierrez, one of the founding fathers of liberation theology. In the same year, the image of Pope John Paul II standing on the tarmac at Managua airport, sternly wagging his finger at Father Ernesto Cardenal, the minister for culture in the Sandanista government, was flashed around the world as an icon of Catholicism's opposition to Marxism. The message was clear: the Holy See would not tolerate what it considered to be wayward theologians.

The following year, representatives of the CDF flew to Bogata, in Colombia, to meet with representatives of the Latin American bishops' conferences. Soon afterwards, the CDF published *Instruction on Certain Aspects of the Theology of Liberation*. While acknowledging that liberation was an important theme in Christianity, it said that some theologies of liberation were not compatible with Catholic teaching. In March 1986 the CDF further developed its critique of liberation theology in the document *Instruction on Christian Freedom and Liberation*.

A leading figure in liberation theology was Leonardo Boff, a Brazilian Franciscan, who argued in his book *Church: Charism and Power* that the Church had exchanged truth for power and security and 'led to the oppression of the faithful'. In 1985 when the CDF issued him with a Notification (a warning) and requested that he maintain a year of silence in order to reflect more deeply on his ideas, there was a furious reaction from some. The ban was eventually lifted, but tensions persisted between Boff and the CDF until he left the priesthood in 1992.

Asked about the Boff case by the BBC's Edward Stourton, Ratzinger said that Boff had not been silenced because of his views on liberation theology.

No, we asked Boff to come to Rome to discuss a particular book he had written, in which he had not just supported liberation theology but had argued that all the Christian churches were just parts of a great whole of the faith. Clearly this was not Catholic teaching. We explained our position and asked him to stop talking about his position for twelve months in order for him to reflect more deeply, and get a greater insight, into the Catholic position on this issue.

However, Ratzinger was not without his supporters and Father Vincent Twomey, who had completed his doctorate under Ratzinger's supervision at Regensburg, strongly defended his reading of liberation theology. 'One could reasonably argue that more might have been accomplished at the political level in Latin America, if liberation theologians had at the outset not been so sceptical of either Catholic social teaching or the political potential of indigenous cultural traditions of piety they later rediscovered, but that is another issue.'

The Ratzinger Report

Ratzinger was not going to let the desire that had surfaced in his youth to share his ideas and insights about God, faith, the Church and the world be stifled because he was now sitting behind a desk. Nor was he going to let his official position or his work at the CDF prevent him from sharing his personal theological insights with the wider world. When he went for a stroll in the evening around the streets near his apartment, stopping to chat with shopkeepers and people who came up to greet him, he might have reflected how his actions against liberation theology were resulting in a caricature image of him in the media. If he couldn't teach in a classroom, then he would find other ways to share his insights. The opportunity came through Jesuit Father Joseph Fessio, another former student of his at Regensburg who, in 1978, had set up Ignatius Press, a Catholic publishing house in San Francisco, USA.

In 1985 Ratzinger agreed to give an extended interview to Italian journalist Vittorio Messori, who wrote for the magazine *Jesu*. They spent three days in a seminary in the small town of Bressanone in the Alps. Messori recalls that Ratzinger declined the home-made biscuits and hot chocolate the nuns brought in each afternoon, preferring a glass of water, and that he wanted to hear some of the jokes doing the rounds in parishes.

The interview appeared in a book entitled *The Ratzinger Report*. In it, Ratzinger revealed his personal thoughts on subjects such as Vatican II, the liturgy, priesthood, the papacy, the role of bishops' conferences, liberalism, relativism, and the permissiveness of modern society, liberation theology, the devil, angels, evangelization and Christian unity. Answering those who claimed he had changed from a liberal to a conservative, he said it was not he that had changed but others. Looking back to Vatican II, he concluded that expectations had been too high among many and that what emerged was not a renewed Church but one whose message and liturgy had been diluted. 'What happened after the Second Vatican Council could itself almost be called a cultural revolution, if you think of the false zeal with which Church buildings were cleaned out and the clergy and religious assumed a new look.'

Not everyone agreed with his analysis. Contributors to the theological journal *Commonweal*, summed up the reaction of many liberals to the report. Monika K. Helwig, suggested, 'This so-called report should be read only by those in sound health, supportive family situations, and deeply satisfying employment.' Another contributor, George G. Higgins, said he found the report dispiriting, its treatment of theologians and episcopal conferences harsh, and its criticisms of North American culture one-sided. 'It is as if the church had been infected by some degenerative malady, some morbid deterioration of the doctrinal tissue, with the fatal germs being carried by certain theologians right through the system.'

The publication of *The Ratzinger Report* threatened to overshadow the Extraordinary Synod being held to mark the twentieth anniversary of Vatican II, leading Cardinal Godfried Daneels of Belgium to complain at a press conference that 'this is not a Synod about a book, it is a Synod about the Council!'

The Curran case

Ratzinger knew that Pope Paul VI's 1968 encyclical *Humane Vitae* didn't have the support of many priests, and even some bishops disagreed with it. But usually their criticisms of it took place in the context of the confessional or private gatherings. Father Charles Curran, a moral theologian at Catholic University of America in Washington D.C., had been one of the first to attack it and he had now decided to do it in his lectures and seminars. Although *Humane Vitae* had not been defined as infallible teaching, Catholics were still expected to assent to it, as it was authoritative teaching from the pope to the whole Church. 'The Church once taught that usury was intrinsically evil, but changed its stance on that. It once tolerated slavery. There is no reason that it cannot change on birth control,' Curran argued.

The CDF wrote to Curran, informing him that he could not teach in the name of the Church and at the same time deny its teaching (the CDF had withdrawn Hans Kung's licence to teach Catholic theology in 1979). The following year, Curran flew to Rome and had an informal meeting with Ratzinger in his office, but the situation was not resolved. Curran returned to Washington and then wrote a letter proposing a compromise measure: he would give up teaching sexual ethics and teach only moral theology. Ratzinger replied that his proposal was unacceptable and that he would advise the university chancellor that Curran was no longer suitable for the post. He was not preventing him from exercising his priesthood or publishing articles, he was only insisting that Curran did what the university hired him to do. Subsequently, in January 1987, Curran was removed from his position and took the university to court for breach of contract. He lost.

As the decade closed, so did the end of another experiment in atheistic ideology. On 10 November, 1989, Ratzinger must have sat glued to the TV as the Berlin Wall – the symbol of the East–West divide – was stormed by cheering crowds from both sides, setting in motion the collapse of the Soviet empire. The Marxist creed that gave birth to liberation theology and the Soviet Union might now have been discredited, but Ratzinger was already turning his attention to the twin ideologies that were now threatening the Church: relativism and secularism.

4 Crisis of Faith

Priesthood

Since Vatican II, an estimated 100,000 priests had resigned. Across Europe and North America, the seminaries were emptying fast, as the view gained ground that priests were really little different from social workers or teachers and, anyway, hadn't the Church always taught that all believers shared in the priesthood by virtue of their common baptism? So what was the point of celibacy?

In 1990 *Shattered Vows: Exodus From the Priesthood* by David Rice, a former Irish priest who left and got married, was published. To research the book he had travelled to a number of countries, including the United States, Holland, Britain, France and Chile, to interview priests who had quit. He painted a grim picture of priests who were lonely, disillusioned and either sleeping around, living with women (often, he claimed, with the tacit approval of their bishop), or practising homosexuals.

This crisis in priestly life was the reason hundreds of bishops from across the world arrived in Rome in October 1990 for the Synod of Bishops on the theme of 'The Formation of Priests in the Circumstances of the Present Day'. Its aim was to discuss and reflect on the formation, nature, spirituality and mission of priests. The Congregation for Catholic Education had, throughout the 1980s, been conducting a series of visitations to seminaries throughout the world and it had produced a number of proposals to reform priestly training.

Priesthood was a topic that figured high on Pope John

Paul's agenda. He had taken to writing annual letters to the 400,000 or so priests around the world on Holy Thursday, which commemorates the institution of the priesthood at the Last Supper, and when he visited a country he always made the point of affirming and encouraging priests in their ministry.

In contrast to the West, in Africa, there was a different type of crisis: seminaries were struggling to cope with the numbers of young men wanting to be priests. Even in the Far East, which, apart from the Philippines, had always been a tough nut for Catholicism to crack, Korea was producing a rich harvest of priestly vocations.

To Catholics, a priest is more than simply a religious minister who leads services on a Sunday and 'hatches, matches and dispatches'. He represents Christ. He does this through administering the Church's sacraments and preaching the Word of God. The priest as a symbol of Christ is seen at its most potent when he changes the bread and wine into the body and blood of Christ during Mass and pronounces the words of absolution in the sacrament of reconciliation (formerly called confession). This is the reason why Catholics trust and respect their priests so much.

Ratzinger had only ever wanted to be a priest, and after nearly 40 years serving the Church he felt very fulfilled. He believed that by freely choosing celibacy above marriage and family life, as he had done, a priest was able to devote all his time to the care of souls. His training in the seminary would equip him with the necessary theological, liturgical and pastoral tools. But, above all, he must be a man of deep faith and prayer. Ratzinger knew that a spiritually healthy priesthood meant a spiritually healthy Church, which was why, along with Dominican Christoph Schönborn, one of his former students at Regensburg, he had set up a house in Rome for the formation of priests. He recognized that some seminaries were not producing priests who were either sufficiently anchored in prayer or on fire with their faith.

When Cardinal Ratzinger stood up to address the bishops seated in front of him in the modern, sloping auditorium, he wasted no time in identifying the cause of the crisis in the priesthood. 'The great number of those who have left the priesthood and the enormous decline in priestly vocations in many countries certainly cannot be attributed to theological causes alone. The extra-ecclesial causes, however, would not have been nearly so influential if the theological foundations of the priestly ministry had not been discredited among many priests and young people,' he said, emphasizing strongly that a priest cannot last in his ministry 'without strong spiritual substance'.

Only men, of course, are allowed to be priests in the Catholic Church. The Catholic position on ordaining women to the priesthood has always been on the grounds that Christ did not call women to be part of his inner group of disciples and that the apostles continued this practice, and that when the priest stands at the altar he represents the person of Christ, so therefore he must be male. This view is shared by the Orthodox Churches and the Ancient Churches of the East.

Feminists

Eight months after Pope John Paul had published the synod's findings in *Pastores Dabo Vobis* (I Shall Give You Shepherds), which struck a positive note, despite the crisis, the Church of England voted at their general synod to break with their 400-year-old tradition and ordain women, a move that not only undid the previous ecumenical dialogue between Canterbury and Rome but also fractured the 70-million strong Anglican Communion.

This was a great victory for the feminist movement that was on the march across Europe and North America. Having breached the walls of Canterbury, the feminists must have thought they could achieve the same success in Rome.

Cardinal Ratzinger perhaps wondered if some of those who attacked the Church for admitting only men to the priesthood concealed another agenda. Because of its teaching about artificial contraception and abortion, the Church angered some feminists who saw it as not just patriarchal but also as an oppressor of women. This was clearly not a view shared by the thousands of young African and Asian Catholic women who opted to enter religious orders each year.

In May 1994 Ratzinger found himself caught up in this issue following Pope John Paul's apostolic letter *Ordinatio Sacerdotalis* (On Reserving Priestly Ordination to Men Alone). It wasn't saying anything new, simply reaffirming Pope Paul VI's 1976 document *Inter Insigniores* (Among the Characteristics), published after the Episcopalian Church in the United States decided to ordain women, which stated that the priesthood was reserved for men and that the Church had no authority to ordain women.

In a commentary on the letter, Ratzinger stated that the teaching about an all-male priesthood was not a matter of Church discipline, like celibacy, but a doctrine. Those campaigning for women to be admitted to the priesthood were unconvinced. Cardinal Martini of Milan reacted to the letter by suggesting that future discussions about women and ministry in the Church should look at the diaconate, which was, he pointed out, not mentioned in the document.

If Ratzinger thought the issue of women's ordination had gone away, he was wrong. In October a bishop sent a *dubium* (a question asking for a response) to the CDF. He wanted to know if the teaching was infallible, a doctrine defined at the First Vatican Council. Ratzinger's reply was that Pope John Paul had stated that the teaching was 'to be held always, everywhere, and by all, as belonging to the deposit of faith'. This only fuelled the controversy even more, with a number of theologians calling into question the Church's teaching on papal infallibility.

The catechism

Vatican II had unwittingly sowed the seeds of much confusion among many about what the Catholic Church actually taught. Some of the issues that had once been very clear now appeared very fuzzy in an increasingly ecumenical and secular climate. Cardinal Ratzinger had been given the task by Pope John Paul of overseeing the publication of the *Catechism of the Catholic Church*, the first universal catechism of the Catholic Church for 400 years. He made Christoph Schönborn the general editor and in 1992, after six years of consultations with bishops around the world, and many drafts, the 700-page compendium was published, first in French and then in English two years later.

It was an immediate hit with Catholics who were hungry for solid teaching. Some theologians criticized it as a too rigid definition of Catholic teaching but Ratzinger, on the other hand, saw it as a much needed clarification and presentation of the authentic teaching of the Church to help Catholics deepen their faith.

In his book *Gospel, Catechesis, Catechism: Sidelights on the Catechism of the Catholic Church*, Ratzinger said that while some Catholics had 'shut out' the book, declaring it a 'fundamental mistake', many others 'had pronounced a very different judgment'. For Ratzinger, those who suffered most from the worst interpretations of Vatican II were people with a simple faith, and they needed his protection.

Salt of the Earth

In 1996 Ratzinger agreed to another extended interview, this time with Peter Seewald, a lapsed Catholic. It was published as *Salt of the Earth* and became a bestseller around the world. One of the many issues Ratzinger talked about was why he had taken a stand against liberation theology. 'Religion must not be turned into the handmaiden of political ideologies. The autonomy of Christianity must be defended against the armed enthusiasts of world revolution, however nobly intentioned they may be,' he explained.

Ratzinger was now portrayed as an autocratic, power-mad figure, dubbed the 'panzer cardinal'. But it was not just the world's media who did this, as best-selling author Piers Paul Read remembers:

I recall going to a meeting in London in 1989 organized by Christian Aid and CIIR [Catholic Institute for International Relations] to discuss the rise of 'oppressive Christianity' in the Third World. The director of the CIIR described how the aid agencies, by exercising a preferential option for the poor had produced an effect on Christianity 'little short of that of the Protestant Reformation', but were now facing a counter-Reformation mounted by right-wing dictators, Protestant sects – and the Vatican! The audience, which included a Catholic bishop, was enthralled. Whenever the name of Ratzinger was mentioned, it produced a jeer.

Aware of the loathing some had for him, there must have been times when Cardinal Ratzinger allowed his mind to wander from the files scattered across his desk to those golden childhood moments in Bavaria when he would set off on a hike with his mother to the Austrian border or go fishing for carp with his brother Georg in the lakes. Whether the brain haemorrhage he suffered in 1991, forcing him to spend several days in hospital, had anything to do with the pressures of the CDF, he never said.

All that had ever mattered to him was the truth; that truth he found in the words of Christ each time he celebrated early morning Mass for students and pilgrims at the nearby Teutonic College before starting work at his office. He believed that his task at the CDF was to protect 'this precious treasure, the faith, with its power to enlighten, from being lost' and to defend those who could not fight back 'against intellectual assault on what sustains their life'.

One God, many faiths?

If Jesus is that truth which reveals the mystery of God, then is it possible that other religious traditions can also be paths of salvation? Could it be that all religions are equally valid ways to God? The question of pluralism had become a hot topic in a shrinking world where people of different faiths encountered each other more and more. In cities in England at one time, you would find a Catholic church, Anglican church and Baptist chapel in the same street. Now you might find they have been joined by a mosque and a Hindu temple. And Eastern traditions in meditation were beginning to impact on traditional Catholic spirituality (the Jesuit college I attended in the early 1980s had a 'Zen chapel' – though none of the students knew what Zen was). The relationship between Christianity and other religions was of particular concern in Asia. Ratzinger acknowledged this when he flew into Hong Kong to give an address entitled 'Christ, Faith and the Challenge of Culture' to the presidents of the Asian bishops' conferences and the heads of their doctrinal commissions in Hong Kong in 1993.

And in an address to the doctrinal commissions of the Latin American bishops' conference at a meeting in Guadalajara, Mexico, in 1996, he warned against relativism creeping into inter-religious dialogue, claiming that 'it also seems necessary to the Christian theology in India to set aside the image of Christ from its exclusive position – which is considered typically Western – in order to place it on the same level as the Indian saving myths. The historical Jesus – it is now thought – is no more the absolute Logos than any other saving figure of history.'

In January 1997 when Father Tissa Balasuriya, an Oblate of Mary working in mainly Buddhist Sri Lanka and the author of *Mary and Human Liberation*, was excommunicated – a very rare event nowadays – for refusing to accept the teaching of the Church on a wide range of issues (it was reported that women priests was the main reason for him being being excluded from communion with the Church).

Speaking to reporters at a press conference, Cardinal Ratzinger with his customary patience clarified the situation. 'It is not exactly true that this theologian was excommunicated because of his position regarding women priests. Rather it was because of other unacceptable positions which touch on the Catholic faith, in particular regarding the doctrine of original sin.' He explained that Father Balasuriya had been invited to sign a profession of faith, but refused, leaving the CDF with no other option than to excommunicate him, but he added that Balasuriya could be received back into communion if he assented to Church doctrine.

The CDF was similarly misreported over the case of Father Jacques Dupuis, a mouse-like Belgian Jesuit in his late seventies, who had spent 36 years working in India before coming to Rome to teach at the Pontifical University. With its 150 dioceses and 14 million Catholics, the Church was still only a minority in a country of around 750 million people. Dupuis' contact with Hindus, Buddhists and Muslims had forced him to ask deep questions about Christian revelation and its relationship to other religions.

The CDF was asked to examine his book *Towards a Christian Theology of Religious Pluralism*. At the heart of Dupuis' theology was the idea that the fullness of revelation will not be totally understood until the end of time and that, while Jesus is the saviour of mankind and the Catholic Church the true Church, God is also at work in other religious traditions. The touchstone for assessing Dupuis' writings was the Vatican II document *Nostra Aetate* (A Declaration on the Relationship of the Church to Non-Christian Religions), which starts out by affirming what Catholicism and other religions share in common and goes on to say, 'the Catholic Church rejects nothing which is true and holy in these religions.'

While the investigation was carried out, Dupuis was suspended from his teaching post and the CDF sent a number of questions for him to answer. The story was leaked to the press and Cardinal Franz König of Vienna, in an article in the Catholic weekly, *The Tablet*, accused the CDF of arrogance and colonialism in its approach to other religions.

Ratzinger was annoyed and responded by writing to *The Tablet*, who published his letter. He defended the CDF's handling of Father Dupuis, saying, '… I fail to understand your statement that our attempt at dialogue implies that the congregation "may well suspect him of directly or indirectly violating the Church's teaching". Such a suspicion was only created by a certain kind of publicity, not by us.'

Meanwhile, the publication by the CDF of the document *Dominus Iesus* (My Lord Jesus) in September 2000 created a further storm. The document had stated, amongst other things, that it was incorrect to refer to 'sister churches' when describing other Christian denominations as this implied there was more than one church. 'Vatican Declares Catholicism Sole Path to Salvation,' yelled the *Los Angeles Times* headline, reflecting most of the media reaction. Although the major theme of the document concerned the role of Christ and the Church in the salvation of non-Christians, the strongest reactions came from Christian leaders and some Catholics. In the view of many of them, *Dominus Iesus* placed a barrier across the road of any future ecumenical progress.

In an interview with the German newspaper *Allgemeine Zeitung*, Ratzinger defended the document, arguing that Christ was uniquely at the centre of God's plan of salvation and that, correctly speaking in the eyes of the Church, only those who were in communion with the apostles, namely the Catholic Church and the the Orthodox Churches and Ancient Churches of the East constituted the Church. Others were Christians, yes, but they were members of 'ecclesiastical communities'. In other words, Ratzinger was stating traditional Catholic teaching that the Bible alone didn't make the Church. This had been a major issue during the Reformation. What defined the Church was its tradition of teaching, which went back to the apostles. The Bible grew out of the Church; not the other way round.

Ratzinger has always argued that the only authentic ecumenical or inter-faith dialogue is that which is built on honesty. In other words, not watering down core beliefs to please the other side. Those who suggested he was anti-Protestant were missing the point. In fact, his outstanding knowledge of the Bible and biblical scholarship was recognized in many Protestant circles, such as the evangelical Howard Centre for Family, Religion and Society who had invited him to New York in 1988 to give their annual Erasmus Lecture.

The Dupuis case reached a conclusion in February 2001 when the CDF issued him with a Notification, stating that his writings contained 'ambiguities and difficulties on important points which could lead a reader to erroneous or harmful opinions'. But, importantly, there was no outright condemnation.

Homosexuality

Catholic teaching about homosexuality was now being openly challenged by some in the Church. Pope John Paul had removed French Bishop Jacques Gaillot from his diocese of Evreux in 1995 for flouting Church teaching about homosexuality, condoms and abortion, and gave him the diocese of Partenia in Algeria. As it had been obsolete since the fifth century, it seemed there would be little chance of him causing any further problems. Gaillot got around this by setting up a 'diocese without borders' on the internet.

In 1977 Sister Jeannine Gramick and Father Robert

Nugent had set up New Ways Ministry in the Archdiocese of Washington to provide pastoral care to homosexuals. Their approach, however, was seen to be inconsistent with Catholic teaching and in 1984 Cardinal James Hickey banned them from working in the archdiocese, and the Congregation for Institutes of Consecrated Life and for Societies of Apostolic Life ordered them to cease their activities. Despite this, Gramick and Nugent continued their work, leading to numerous complaints, calls and requests for clarification from bishops and others in the United States of America. In 1988 the Holy See established a commission to study their work. It paid particular attention to their book *Building Bridges: Gay and Lesbian Reality and the Catholic Church*.

As the main issues were doctrinal, the case was eventually sent to the CDF. Cardinal Ratzinger's attempts to persuade the two Americans to get back in line failed. The publication in 1995 of their book *Voices of Hope: A Collection of Positive Catholic Writings on Gay and Lesbian Issues* had made it clear that there was no change in their opposition to fundamental elements of the Church's teaching. The case rumbled on and the paperwork mounted. Finally, in July 1999, Gramick and Nugent were issued with a Notification. 'Crushing the pastors' ran the headline on the front page of *The Tablet* the following week.

Cardinal Bertone, Ratzinger's number two, explained the decision about Gramick and Nugent. 'Persons who are struggling with homosexuality, no less than any others, have the right to receive the authentic teaching of the church from those who minister to them.' For all their good intentions and genuine pastoral motives, Gramick and Nugent were still expected to teach people what the Church taught about homosexuality and homosexuals, not what *they* thought. Catholic teaching makes a clear distinction between the homosexual act and homosexual activity. The first is a sin – like adultery – and the second is a tendency whose psychological origins the Church admits it cannot explain.

Mystics

Alleged apparitions, mystical experiences, miracles and other strange phenomena litter the pages of Catholic history. The Church always takes a very cautious approach when it hears of such cases, stressing that whether or not these events are true, they add nothing to the essentials of Catholic belief.

Cardinal Ratzinger found himself examining the case of Vassula Ryden, born in Egypt to Greek parents, and who claimed to have been receiving messages from Jesus since he first appeared to her in 1985 while she was living in Bangladesh. Her writings have been translated into over 40 languages and her 'apostolic call' (movement) known as True Life in God, which she runs from her home in Washington D.C., has given her a large international following that includes theologians, priests and even bishops.

However, others, worried about Ryden's growing popularity in some Catholic circles, contacted the CDF. Having carefully studied the evidence, in October 1995 Ratzinger decided to issue her with a Notification. At the time it was widely reported that he had condemned her, but this was incorrect, as he explained in an interview published in the magazine *30 Days* in January 1999:

> No, the Notification is a warning, not a condemnation. From the strictly procedural point of view, no person may be condemned without a trial and without being given the opportunity to air their views first. What we say is that there are many things which are not clear. There are some debatable apocalyptic elements and ecclesiological aspects which are not clear. Her writings contain many good things but the grain and the chaff are mixed up. That is why we invited Catholic faithful to view it all with a prudent eye and to measure it by the yardstick of the constant faith of the Church.

Ryden voluntarily submitted more of her writings for examination and in 2004 Cardinal Ratzinger wrote to the presidents of the bishops' conferences of France, Switzerland, Uruguay, the Philippines and Canada, who had expressed particular concern over Ryden, saying that he was leaving it up to them to decide whether they supported her or not.

It is possible that Ratzinger had in mind Sister Faustina Kowalska, a Polish mystic who died in 1938, claiming to have received private revelations telling her that she had been called to renew devotion to God's mercy. She had recorded her mystical experiences in a diary and had later been investigated by one of Ratzinger's predecessors. She was cleared. In 2000 she was canonized by Pope John Paul.

God and the world

In early 2000, sitting in the back of the car as Alfredo, his chauffeur, skilfully negotiated the steep, narrow track that spiralled up the mountain, Cardinal Ratzinger must have been looking forward to a few days of quiet and an opportunity to spend time in prayer at the Monastery of Monte Cassino, near Naples. St Benedict had died here in AD 550, leaving behind his Rule, which was to shape Western monasticism and European civilization. The monastery had been destroyed more than once down the centuries, but each time it had been rebuilt. The purpose of Ratzinger's visit was to share his insights and thoughts about God with journalist Peter Seewald, who had conducted the interview that became the book *Salt of the Earth*.

One of the areas Seewald wanted to explore with Ratzinger was his spiritual life. When he asked him how God spoke to him, he replied:

God speaks quietly. But he gives us all kinds of signs. In retrospect, especially, we can see that he has given us a little nudge through a friend, through a book, or through what we see as failure – even through 'accidents'. Life is actually full of these silent indications. If I remain alert, then slowly they piece together a consistent whole, and I begin to feel how God is guiding me.

This kind of listening out for God was crucial in learning how to talk to God, he explained.

Slowly one learns to spell out God's letters, to speak his language, and – if still inadequately – to understand God. Gradually, then, one will become able to pray for oneself and to talk with God, at first in a very childlike way – in a certain sense we always remain like that – but then more and more in one's own words...

Wherever one person does something good for another, there God is especially near. Whenever someone opens himself for God in prayer, then he enters into his own special closeness.

In Jesus, God made himself little and challenged human pride with love. Jesus shows us what man ought to be, how he ought to live, and what we ought to work towards.

The new millennium

Throughout the 1990s the Church had been busy preparing itself to celebrate the 2,000 years since the birth of Christ and its entry into the third millennium, and special synods had been held in Rome for the Americas, Europe, Lebanon, Asia, Africa and Oceania. But, according to *Catholic World News*, Ratzinger had 'reservations' about the large number of public celebrations scheduled in Rome. Speaking to reporters at the close of a conference of lay movements, he said that he was not opposed to the celebrations, but would be uncomfortable in the midst of a 'permanently celebratory structure', pointing out that one journal had listed 240 celebrations for the jubilee.

During the jubilee year, over 20 million people streamed through the holy door in St Peter's Basilica. The last special event of the celebrations was a Mass for actors, film directors, funfair workers, jugglers and circus performers and others in the entertainment industry. The largest celebration was World Youth Day, held at the sprawling Tor Vergat university campus on the edge of the city, when an estimated one million young Catholics turned out.

Yet, behind this celebration, some saw a divided Church about to enter the third millennium. Father Ian Ker, writing in *The Catholic Herald* in 1999, observed:

> I think it is time to say that there is a very widespread sense of disillusion among Catholics about the situation in which the Church now finds herself. Conservatives, while accepting the teachings of the Second Vatican Council, deplore many of the things that have happened since the Council. Liberals, on the other hand, resent that there have not been more changes of the kind that they regard as legitimate developments of Vatican II.

Cardinal Ratzinger had now served 20 years as prefect of the CDF. Back in 1996 he had talked publicly about retiring, but Pope John Paul, unwilling to lose him, persuaded him to stay on. To mark this milestone, in November 2001 he gave an interview to Vatican Radio.

Q: How is it possible today to have authority on matters of faith?
Ratzinger: It is certainly a difficult task, in part because the concept of authority no longer exists. The fact that an authority can decide anything today seems incompatible

with the freedom to do what one wishes.

It is also difficult because many general tendencies of our time are opposed to the Catholic faith: what is sought is a simplified view of the world. Therefore, Christ cannot be the Son of God but a myth, a great human personality, because God could not have accepted Christ´s sacrifice, God could not be a cruel God.

In a word, there are many ideas that are opposed to Christianity, and many truths of the faith would have to be reformulated to be adapted to the man of today. However, I must say that many people also thank the Church for continuing to be a force that expresses the Catholic faith and offers a foundation on which to live and die. And this is something that consoles me.

Q: Your twenty years in the Vatican congregation are closely connected to this pontificate. What are your most intense memories?

Ratzinger: My most intense memories are linked to the meetings with the Pope in the great trips and great drama of the theology of liberation, when we sought the just way. Then comes the Holy Father's ecumenical commitment: that search for a great opening of the Church while, at the same time, not losing its identity.

Ordinary meetings with the Pope are, perhaps, the most beautiful experience, because we speak heart to heart and feel our common intention to serve the Lord. We also see how the Lord helps us to find companionship on our way, as I don't do anything on my own.

This is very important: One must not take a personal decision alone, but with great collaboration. And this, always in the way of communion with the Pope, who has a great vision of the future. He confirms and leads me in my way.

Q: Could you describe yourself?

Ratzinger: It is impossible to paint a self-portrait; it is difficult to judge oneself. I can only say that I come from a very simple family, very humble, and that is why I feel more like a simple man than a cardinal. I have my home in Germany, in a small village, with people who work in agriculture, in craftsmanship, and there I feel at home. I also try to be like this in my work: I don´t know if I succeed, I don't dare judge myself. I always remember very affectionately the profound goodness of my father and my mother and, naturally, for me, goodness means the capacity to say 'no,' because a goodness that allows everything, does the other no good. At times goodness means having to say 'no,' and run the risk of contradiction. These are my criteria, this is my origin; the rest must be judged by others.

Many, it seemed, had already formed their judgment. Ratzinger was nothing more than a tyrant who stood for a Church that was anachronistic and out of touch. Father Joseph McCabe, an American who worked in the Vatican and is now working in Siberia, painted a different picture.

> On my very last day working for the Holy See, in January of 2001, I was sitting in a meeting with the heads of various Congregations and their assistants as an important issue was being discussed – one that I had worked on for the last three years I was in Rome. Cardinal Ratzinger had obviously read the report under discussion from beginning to end and he had amazingly incisive questions, drawing out some of the material to its logical conclusion. One could not but feel graced by this theological mind at work. He could see things that others would perhaps miss or gloss over. But what impressed me more was his approach to these complex theological issues: he came to each question with a firm grasp of the biblical and theological issue but also with a deep concern for the pastoral implications. This was the only time we ever spoke, but I remember it well

because one cannot but remember meeting this quiet, intelligent and holy man.

He was also impressed at how thoroughly Cardinal Ratzinger did his work when assessing the cases he had to study. He added that the documents that the CDF produced contained the footnotes and references which showed that the situation had been considered from many angles.

Cardinal Desmond Connell of Dublin echoed those thoughts.

'I have been at meetings over the years where he has presided and he is most courteous as a chairman. He never interrupts anyone and he respects the views expressed by others. I've also known him as a bishop because I've had problems to bring to his attention, and he has always given me every support.'

Disagreements

Having had a public disagreement over inter-religious dialogue a few years before with Cardinal König, Ratzinger was now being publicly challenged by fellow German Cardinal Walter Kasper, his opposite number at the Pontifical Council for Promoting Christian Unity. They had known each other for 40 years and they had both been part of the group that founded *Communio*. Like Ratzinger, Kasper had trailed a glittering academic career, at the universities of Munster and Tübingen, and then, for a brief spell, in the United States before being appointed Bishop of Rottenburg-Stuttgart.

They had clashed, however, in 1993 after Kasper put his name to a pastoral letter encouraging divorced Catholics who had remarried in a civil ceremony to return to the sacraments. And he had publicly criticized *Dominus Iesus* for 'lacking sensitivity' and being 'too brief', though he made it clear he was commenting on its tone, not its content.

In 2001 they undertook a public debate through the pages of several Catholic journals over the question of which came first: the universal Church or the local Church? Cardinal Kasper argued that the local takes precedence. Ratzinger said the opposite was true. As their articles appeared, each countering the other, they took on the appearance of two enemy battleships patrolling in disputed waters, circling each other and occasionally firing warning shots, but never quite ready for an all-out attack. Behind what appeared to be an academic debate are major questions about the Church, the authority of local bishops and, by definition, the authority of the pope.

Ratzinger and Pope John Paul, too, sometimes saw things differently. In January 2002 Ratzinger joined a colourful group of native American Indians, Buddhists, representatives of traditional African religions, rabbis, mullahs and Christian leaders who clambered on board the seven-carriage train at the Vatican's own railway station (one of the few occasions it has been used in recent years) for the journey north to the medieval hill town of Assisi, where St Francis had turned his back on wealth and set out with a group of followers to preach the gospel.

This was the third Day of Prayer for World Peace called by Pope John Paul, this time in response to the attack on the World Trade Center in New York on 11 September 2001. The group was together to pray, not as the media reported, to pray *together*. A subtle but crucial theological distinction. Ratzinger was reported to have remarked, 'This cannot be the model.' If this is true, then it might have been because the Franciscans removed crosses and other religious objects from some rooms in a convent to avoid offending some of the representatives. He would have seen that as a distortion of genuine inter-faith dialogue which, in his view, had to be built on respect for differences, not hiding them.

The Milingo affair

Bishops forming liaisons with women is rare but not unknown (in recent times Eamon Casey in Ireland and Roddy Wright in Scotland had both seen their names splashed across the front pages for the wrong reasons), but even Ratzinger must have been flabbergasted by the bizarre shenanigans of 71-year-old Archbishop Emeritus Emmanuel Milingo of Lusaka. The flamboyant Zambian prelate had been a controversial figure for years over his use of exorcism in what he called Healing Masses, which drew huge crowds. This had led the Holy See to bring him from Africa to Rome. Cardinal Carlo Martini of Milan and other Italian bishops soon started to complain about his behaviour – he performed publicly as a singer and dancer and produced two albums of his songs – but even they must have been astounded at the events that unfolded in front of the world's media.

To everyone's astonishment, in May 2001 Milingo announced that he had married 43-year-old Maria Sung, an acupuncturist from South Korea, at a mass wedding – Blessing Ceremony – in a hotel ballroom in New York. Presiding over it was the Reverend Sun Myung Moon, founder of The Family Federation for World Peace and Unification, better known as the Moonies, and his wife. Moon had started the church after claiming Jesus had appeared to him in 1936, when he was 16, and asked him to complete his mission. The papacy had thrown up some meaty stories down the centuries, but it had probably never seen anything like this. In a press statement, Milingo said, 'The same living God who has led me to a life of service to His church and His people, has now led me to work with the honourable Reverend and Mrs Sun Myung Moon.'

There might have been amusement around the world, and Hollywood script writers might have been busy bashing away at their keyboards, but behind the doors of the CDF urgent discussions were taking place about how to deal with this embarrassing episcopal soap opera. In July 2001

Ratzinger sent a letter to Milingo. It was straight to the point: if, by 20 August, he didn't separate immediately from Maria Sung, sever all links with the Moonies, and declare publicly fidelity to the discipline of celibacy and the teaching of the pope, he would be excommunicated.

The letter worked, eventually. After initially insisting that he had no intention of leaving his wife, and asking to be released from celibacy, Milingo left Maria following a meeting with Pope John Paul on 7 August at his summer residence of Castel Gandolfo in the hills south of Rome. The CDF threat of excommunication was immediately lifted.

However, with claims that the Vatican had kidnapped, drugged or brainwashed him, Sung then turned up in Rome and staged a hunger strike in St Peter's Square. Ratzinger must have been shaking his head and wondering what was to come next. At the end of August, Milingo and Sung then held a press conference at which they announced their separation. Following a year-long retreat in Argentina, he then took the CDF's advice and went to live at a centre for spirituality at Zagarolo, near Rome, where he was allowed to resume his ministry. But, amidst reports that he felt under Vatican surveillance at the centre, in 2003 he flew to his native Zambia, despite opposition from both the CDF and the Zambian bishops' conference. The story continues.

Sins of the fathers

But the Milingo affair was only a slight tremor compared to the earthquake caused by the clergy sex abuse crisis that was to rock the Church. Accusations against priests and religious of sexual abuse had started to appear in the media with alarming frequency throughout the 1990s. Catholics, especially those who had traditionally placed priests on pedestals, were shocked and appalled.

In many countries priests and even some bishops were accused of sexually abusing minors, and some were jailed. In

1996 Bishop Hubert O'Connor of Canada, a principal of a boarding school, was imprisoned for sexually assaulting two teenage girls. Cardinal Hans Hermann Groer of Vienna resigned in 1995 following molestation claims from former seminarians. And in 1999 Father Sean Fortune, who was facing 29 charges of sex abuse against young boys, committed suicide at his home in County Wexford, Ireland.

But it was in the United States where the sexual abuse story really exploded, as in early 2002 one story after another emerged of priests accused of sexual abuse and then of dioceses, such as Tucson and Boston, paying out millions to victims in out-of-court settlements. American Catholics were outraged by the revelations, and their anger turned on the hierarchy, some of whom they felt had been engaged in a cover-up. Bishop Anthony O'Connell of Palm Beach, Archbishop Rembert Weakland of Milwaukee and Cardinal Bernard Law of Boston all later resigned.

As many newspaper columnists pointed out, the cause of the crisis was clearly celibacy: it is unnatural, therefore some priests target children to release their sexual frustrations. As most of the victims were young boys, the Church's attitude to homosexuality was discussed at length. You didn't have to listen very hard to hear the sniggers emanating from many quarters.

In April 2002 12 American cardinals were summoned to Rome for a crisis meeting with Pope John Paul, Ratzinger and other top curial officials. Topics discussed included the reassignment of priests who have abused children, the observance of celibacy, seminary screening and formation, and the high percentage of homosexuals in the priesthood. Describing sexual abuse as 'an appalling sin in the eyes of God', the pope said 'There is no place in the priesthood and religious life for those who would harm the young.' He admitted that some bishops had made decisions that turned out to be wrong, but stressed that the vast majority of priests and religious served the Church faithfully.

Some months later, Ratzinger came under fire when he told Zenit, the Catholic news agency, there was a media campaign to discredit the whole Church for the actions of a few.

> In the Church, priests also are sinners. But I am personally convinced that the constant presence in the press of the sins of Catholic priests, especially in the United States, is a planned campaign, as the percentage of these offences among priests is not higher than in other categories, and perhaps it is even lower. In the United States, there is constant news on this topic, but less than one per cent of priests are guilty of acts of this type. The constant presence of these news items does not correspond to the objectivity of the information nor to the statistical objectivity of the facts.

Ratzinger was not alone in this view. Professor Philip Jenkins – a non-Catholic – of Pennsylvania State University and author of *Pedophiles and Priests: Anatomy of a Contemporary Crisis*, published in 2001, says:

> My research of cases over the past twenty years indicates no evidence whatever that Catholic or other celibate clergy are any more likely to be involved in misconduct or abuse than clergy of any other denomination – or indeed, than non-clergy. However determined news media may be to see this affair as a crisis of celibacy, the charge is just unsupported.

Ratzinger's analysis of the sexual abuse scandal was simple: it was not celibacy at the root of the problem; it was a crisis in faith, or sin. In other words, if priests were living a life of deep faith and prayer none of this would have happened. As he had said at the Synod of Bishops in 1990, a priest 'without strong spiritual substance cannot last in his ministry'.

Pope John Paul had lived out his priesthood in a spirit of prayer, faith and service. Over the previous 24 years he and Cardinal Ratzinger had formed a close bond as they battled together both to maintain the unity of the Church and make its message relevant to the modern age. But, as 2005 began, it was evident that John Paul's health was deteriorating rapidly and the media were already talking about his successor. Whoever he turned out to be, he would be facing even bigger challenges in the future.

5 The New Benedictine Age

Filled with the Spirit

Pope Benedict XVI moved serenely and silently, gently laying both hands on the head of each of 21 men kneeling in a semicircle around the sanctuary of St Peter's Basilica, below the colossal canopy supported by four 'barley-sugar' columns. These new priests – from nine countries, including Uruguay, Angola, Ireland, Italy and Romania – would be messengers of the gospel of Christ to a world that was becoming, increasingly, indifferent and even hostile to it. Nevertheless, Benedict believed this same world had never been in more need of the meaning and hope only God could provide it with.

It was Pentecost Sunday, which marks the birth of the Church some 2,000 years ago in Jerusalem when the Acts of the Apostles records that what seemed like tongues of fire rested on the heads of the disciples of Jesus. Then, filled with the Holy Spirit, apostle Peter proclaimed the message of salvation to people from every part of the ancient world.

Dressed in the traditional red vestments of Pentecost, Pope Benedict spoke of the Church of the twenty-first century.

> The Church must always become anew that which she already is: she must open the frontiers between peoples and break down the barriers between classes and races. In her, no one can be forgotten or scorned... The wind and the fire of the Holy Spirit must ceaselessly open the frontiers that we human

beings continue to build between ourselves.

Only in forgiveness is true renewal of the world achieved... Nothing can improve in the world, if evil is not overcome. And evil can be overcome only through forgiveness. This forgiveness can only come through God if it is to be a forgiveness that does not remove evil only with words, but that really transforms it.

That the world is in need of transforming, Pope Benedict is in no doubt. By taking the name Benedict he recalled Pope Benedict XV, who was elected when Europe was on the eve of the First World War. His efforts to bring peace and reconciliation failed, but he took the lead in bringing aid and relief to its victims, especially children. He is also remembered as someone who sought to heal the divisions in the Church as a result of Pius X's crusade against theologians, biblical scholars and others whom he considered to be diluting Catholic teaching to accommodate modern ideas.

The name Benedict also recalls St Benedict of Nursia, co-patron saint of Europe and the founder of Western monasticism, which provided the vehicle for Christianity to help bring Europe out of the Dark Ages. Pope Benedict XVI sees him as 'a fundamental reference point for European unity and a powerful reminder of the indispensable Christian roots of his culture and civilization.' And he seems to think that we might be teetering on the verge of another Dark Age.

Although the Rule of Benedict was written primarily for monasteries, Pope Benedict insists its advice about things such as prayer, work, discipline, leisure, food, hospitality, and caring for the young, the sick and the elderly is as relevant in the modern world as it was when first written 1500 years ago. He says:

Time and time again, our world so easily finds its corrective in the Benedictine rule, since it offers the fundamental human attitudes and virtues needed for a life of inner balance, those that are requisite for social life – and for the maturity of the individual... We can see here, in the Rule of St Benedict, how nothing that is truly human ever becomes old-fashioned... This is a rule that springs from what is truly human, and it was able to formulate what was truly human because it looked out and listened beyond what is human and perceived the divine. Man becomes really human when he is touched by God.

In his homily to the vast crowd at his installation mass, Benedict spoke about his role as a shepherd in the desert. Showing a pastoral concern that surprised his critics, he went on to talk about the deserts of poverty, hunger, thirst, abandonment, loneliness, of destroyed love, of God's darkness and 'the emptiness of souls no longer aware of their dignity or the goal of human life'.

These 'internal deserts' he identifies will shape his thinking and the decisions he makes for a Church of 1.1 billion Catholics, over half of whom live in the Third World. Yet his vision of the world is not confined to Catholics. Over 80 per cent of the planet's population follow other faiths or subscribe to no religion at all. As the successor of St Peter, Pope Benedict sees his task as trying to lead all people into a relationship with God, convinced that 'a kind of memory, a recollection of God' is innate in each human being, but that it needs to be awakened.

Secularism and relativism

In 1978 when Pope John Paul took office he set his sights on confronting atheistic Communism in the East. For Benedict, as he said at St Scholastica's monastery in Subiaco on the night before John Paul died, it is the twin evils of secularism and relativism in the West that pose a danger to the future of mankind.

Secularism says that society should be ordered without God, if indeed he exists, while relativism says that if there is a god then all religions are equally valid ways to him. Both ideologies gained currency in the eighteenth-century Enlightenment when long-held Christian ideas about humankind and the world were abandoned in favour of a philosophy based on science and reason, and a sense of the sacred began to disappear.

Pope Benedict believes that life is a gift from God, who is revealed in the person of Jesus Christ, that the world is caught in a cosmic battle between forces of good and evil, and that moral truths are not something to be decided by the majority, but that they have a divine origin and are therefore eternal. As Professor John Haldane succinctly puts it, 'It is more comfortable to deny that there is sin than to repent and reform.'

Many in the West have abandoned this traditional Christian view of the world, believing instead that morality should change with the times. They claim that absolute rights and absolute wrongs no longer exist, but are relative to an individual's particular situation. If there is a god, the argument goes, then we cannot really know anything of importance about that god. One person's god is as valid as another's.

Following St Augustine, Benedict sees the world not in terms of a struggle between belief and unbelief but as one between love of God and self-sacrifice and denial of God and self-love. Looking at high-tech, consumerist Western society, he sees the creation of an illusion of 'a beauty that is deceptive and false, a dazzling beauty that does not bring human beings out of themselves to open them to the ecstasy of rising to the heights, but indeed locks them entirely into themselves.'

His memory of the horrors of Nazism has been a powerful factor in his thinking.

> It seems to me that we need to rediscover that even the political and economic spheres have need of a moral responsibility, a responsibility that is born in the heart of every man and in the final analysis has to do with the presence or absence of God. I believe we have the capacity and the strength for this rediscovery. A society in which God is absolutely absent self-destructs. We saw this in the totalitarian regimes of the last century.

Behind all the talk of freedom in the West, Benedict sees a worrying trend to stifle religious freedom.

> The dictatorship of opinion is growing, and anyone who doesn't share the prevailing opinion is excluded... Any future anti-Christian dictatorship would probably be much more subtle than anything we have known until now. It will appear to be friendly to religion, but on the condition that its own models of behaviour and thinking not be called into question.

While praising the ecology movement, he notes a mentality in it that denies the spiritual dimension to human beings. 'They crusade with an understandable and also legitimate passion against the pollution of the environment, whereas man's self-pollution of his soul continues to be treated as one of the rights of his freedom.' A freedom that leads man out of relationship with God is a 'caricature of freedom', in Benedict's view.

Europe

Nowhere have secularism and relativism been embraced more enthusiastically than Europe, once the heart of Christendom. When the European Union's constitution was agreed in 2004, it made no explicit reference to God or Christianity. In the words of the writer Clifford Longley, Europe is fast becoming the Church's 'lost continent'.

Yet the secular relativism experiment in Europe has failed to deliver the better society it promised. The pursuit of wealth and pleasure has gone hand in hand with soaring divorce rates (as Pope Paul VI predicted), fractured families, and an anxiety and restlessness often leading to drug and alcohol abuse. Promiscuity, homosexual practice and pornography, once considered morally wrong, are now widely accepted and seen as proof of a liberated society. A report in 2005 from the University of Aberdeen claimed that some GPs in Britain were prescribing the contraceptive pill to girls as young as 10. Elsewhere, the Christian concept of human life was being threatened by stem cell research, embryo research, cloning, abortion, in vitro fertilization and euthanasia.

Benedict does not subscribe to the optimistic Western view that history always progresses, arguing that it moves in circles rather than in a straight line. This can be seen with the way that the so-called sexual liberation of the 1960s has turned sex into a commodity, he says.

In Huxley's famous futuristic novel *Brave New World*, we see a vision of a coming world in which sexuality is something completely detached from procreation. He had good reason to expect this, and its human tragedy is fully explored. In this world, children are planned and produced in a laboratory in a regulated fashion.

For all Pope John Paul's charisma and travels, he was unable to halt the advance of secularism and relativism on the

Catholic Church in Europe. There are now just 12 seminarians for every 100 priests. In the last 40 years, the Church has witnessed a greying and diminishing clergy; dwindling congregations; a missing 18–30 generation; the merger of parishes; the virtual disappearance of the sacrament of reconciliation (confession) in some places; empty rooms in seminary corridors; convents up for sale and religious orders on the verge of folding up; and financial crises.

In England and Wales (following Pope Benedict's election, his books shot into the bestseller lists around the world, while Britain preferred titles such as *Jamie's Dinners* and *You are What You Eat*), only one in four million Catholics still attend Mass regularly. The Capuchins pulled out of Peckham, one of the most deprived parts of London, on the centenary of their arrival, and in 2004, the Jesuits decided to close Campion House College, which had produced 1,500 priests in its 90-year history. Catholic schools are seen to be some of the most successful in the country, yet their fruits are not to be found at Mass on a Sunday morning.

In France, the number of diocesan priests has halved since 1980 and infant baptisms have declined significantly. The Church in Ireland, whose 'priest factories' once served 'the missions', is facing financial problems after paying out £6.1 million in compensation claims to victims of clerical abuse. In Benedict's homeland, Cardinal Georg Sterzinsky is closing or merging half his parishes in Berlin to pay off a £110 million debt to creditors.

The picture in traditionally Catholic Spain looks little more encouraging, according to Jose Ignacio Viton, a Jesuit professor of theology at Pontificia Comillas University in Madrid. He said, 'In the majority of churches, you find old people, and only a few young people. You will find classical concerts. You will find people visiting for the art. But not anymore a place for prayer.'

Father Timothy Radcliffe, the tousled-haired English theologian who was once head of the Dominican order, puts it like this, 'We have lost confidence in any story that can be told about the future of humanity, and so we are more concerned with our own individual story. Does my life lead anywhere? The religion of modern Europe is a pilgrim faith, but does the journey have a final goal, or are we going nowhere?'

Third World

The prosperity of the West, of course, comes at the expense of the Third World, but it is here that Catholicism is thriving. Less than a quarter of Catholics now live in Europe. In the last 25 years the number of Catholics in Africa has tripled from around 55 million to almost 144 million, 17 per cent of the continent's population. Asia and Latin America have also seen rapid growth. In a reversal of 100 years ago, priests from these parts of the world are now being sent to evangelize Europe.

The Church here is facing different challenges to the West, such as poverty, disease, especially AIDS and malaria, a lack of basic health and education services, social injustice and civil war. In Zimbabwe, Archbishop Pius Ncube has stood up to dictator Robert Mugabe, while in East Timor Bishop Carlos Ximenes Belo was awarded the Nobel Prize for Peace for his efforts to bring peace between the Indonesian government and guerrillas. In Sudan, caught up in civil war, famine and ruled by a hardline Muslim government, Cardinal Wako Zubeir provides inspiring leadership to a Catholic Church that has doubled in members in 20 years. Some Catholics pay the ultimate price for their fidelity to the gospel, such as Sister Dorothy Stang, an American missionary, whom, in 2004, was shot dead for defending the rights of farmers in Brazil's Amazon rainforest.

Given that Christianity's main base has shifted from Europe to the Third World, Benedict is aware that solid catechesis is necessary for the Church to continue to be fruitful in these lands. He knows that they, too, in an age of satellite TV and the internet, are under attack from a secular and relativist value system. Some seminaries in Africa might well be full, but one of his biggest challenges will be to make sure that the kind of fossilization that happened in the Church in Europe does not happen in the Third World. And, of course, he will take up from where John Paul left off in putting pressure on Western governments to come up with a new approach to trade, aid and debt in Africa.

Universal and local Church

There has been disquiet amongst some bishops' conferences and theologians over what they see as an unhealthy centralization of decision making in the Vatican. This kind of tension is nothing new, going back to disputes in the Early Church between Peter and Paul over whether Gentiles had to accept Jewish customs when they became Christians. Those such as Cardinal Walter Kasper, prefect of the Pontifical Council for Promoting Christian Unity, would like to see more decisions made at the local level, which is known as collegiality. One bishop famously quipped that on his visits to Rome he felt that the curia 'treated him like an altar boy'.

The disagreement amongst American bishops in 2004 over the then Cardinal Ratzinger's letter about whether presidential candidate John Kerry should receive communion because of his pro-abortion views highlights some of the tensions that sometimes exist between the Holy See and a local church, which, in the case of the United States, is a very divided one.

In the week following Pope Benedict's election, page three of the *National Catholic Reporter* provided a snapshot of some of the problems amongst the 67 million Catholics in the United States. Archbishop Timothy Dolan's proposal to introduce the Clergy Advocacy and Monitoring Program, which would conduct surprise inspections of clergy residences, was withdrawn after protests from priests in Milwaukee. A California jury awarded two brothers nearly $2 million for being sexually abused by a priest when they were altar boys. Bishop Richard Malone announced that the 135 parishes in Portland diocese would be grouped into 27 clusters, with each assigned one priest. Meanwhile, outside Holy Name Cathedral in Chicago, protesters gathered carrying signs that read, 'Priestly people come in both sexes!'

Cardinal Francis George of Chicago summed up the Church in the United States like this:

> We are at a turning point in the life of the Church…
> Liberal Catholicism is an exhausted project. Essentially
> a critique, even a necessary critique at one point in
> our history, it is now parasitical on a substance that
> no longer exists. It has shown itself unable to pass on
> the faith in its integrity and inadequate, therefore, in
> fostering the joyful self-surrender called for in
> Christian marriage, in consecrated life, in ordained
> priesthood. It no longer gives life.

The public debate between Cardinal Kasper might suggest that Pope Benedict will introduce little change in the relationship between the Holy See and local churches. While he sees the papacy as having predominance over local churches, he does say, 'Everything should not take place by way of committees' and admits the Church is weighed down under 'over-institutionalisation' of its 'institutional power'. This could suggest that the local bishops' conferences might be given more say in handling certain matters.

Christian unity

In his homily in the Sistine Chapel at the end of the conclave Pope Benedict made it clear that Christian unity will be a priority for him, though he has said in the past that he thinks complete unity is unlikely. He said that 'concrete gestures are required to penetrate souls and move consciences' and that there is an urgent need for 'purification of memory'. Yet the issues of women priests and gay bishops are serious stumbling blocks along the ecumenical path.

Pope John Paul famously said that the Church 'breathed with two lungs', East and West, but he was unable to make as much progress with the Orthodox churches as he had wished. What lies behind the 1,000 year split between Constantinople and Rome is not issues such as women priests, gay bishops or the sacraments, as is the case with Protestant churches, but rather the primacy of the pope and his exercise of authority.

That Russia, too, like much of Eastern Europe (despite the packed trains from Cracow that snaked their way to Rome for John Paul's funeral), is facing a rise in secularism may help to bring the Catholic and Orthodox worlds closer. However, tensions involving the Greek Catholic Church in western Ukraine will have to be resolved. From the windows of the Russian Orthodox Patriarchate in Moscow, this land appears as their 'canonical territory' and the presence of Catholics as an act of proselytization.

Paradoxically, Benedict, being a non-Slav, might be more successful than John Paul in creating a better understanding and closer cooperation between Catholics and Orthodox. Prior to his papacy, the Patriarch of Constantinople had awarded him the Golden Cross of Mount Athos for his contribution to fostering closer ties between Orthodoxy and Catholicism.

Other religions

Pope John Paul made unprecedented efforts to heal the historic wounds and misunderstandings between Christians, Jews and Muslims, becoming the first pope to visit a mosque and a synagogue and issuing an apology for the sins committed by the Church against the Jews. Pope Benedict says the Jews 'still have a special place in God's plans', adding that the reunification of Jews and Christians as one chosen people is in God's hands.

With the rise in terrorism from extremist Islamic groups and attacks on Christians in countries such as Nigeria and Pakistan, Islam will present a tougher challenge than Judaism. While Pope John Paul's support for the rights of the Palestinians and his opposition to the US-led invasion of Iraq impressed the Muslim world, Benedict's objection to Turkey joining the European Union on the grounds that it will damage European culture has not gone down well. At the same time, he has defended Muslims against the Islamophobia that has risen amongst some in Europe.

The Pontifical Council for Inter-religious Dialogue, headed by Englishman Archbishop Michael Fitzgerald, is in the forefront of building bridges with other religions and sends greetings to Buddhists, Hindus, Sikhs and others on their special holy days. While Benedict is cautious in his approach to non-monotheistic faiths, fearing that such dialogue can make Christ out to be just one of a number of deities, he has, nevertheless, spoken of how 'something of the light of God shines through in the great religions of the world'. China and its persecuted Catholic Church, split into two by the Communist government, might well be a priority for Benedict.

Faith

Pope Benedict sees himself as 'a humble worker in the vineyard of the Lord'. He once spoke of how the vineyards around Frascati, the wine town in southern Italy, only bear fruit if they are pruned once a year. He sees this as a parable of human existence and the Church. 'If the courage of pruning is lacking, only leaves still grow.' By this he means that each person, and society, needs to constantly examine how they live in accordance with God's laws.

Despite being a heavyweight theologian who has written over 50 books and countless articles, he says that what God asks for is a simple faith rather than great knowledge. Speaking to the Spanish newspaper *La Razon*, Cardinal Joachim Meisner of Cologne said of Pope Benedict that 'He has the intelligence of 12 professors and is as pious as a child on the day of his first communion.'

Benedict says of faith, 'The core of faith rests upon accepting being loved by God, and therefore to believe is to say Yes, not only to him, but to creation, to creatures, above all to men, to try and see the image of God in each person and thereby become a lover.'

Along with a simplicity in faith, he believes that joy is essential. He says, 'Today, Christians are often weary of their faith and regard it as heavy baggage that they drag along but they really aren't that joyful about it.' He is not talking about a joy brought about by the Western consumer lifestyle but of a joy derived from the knowledge that Christ has redeemed the world through his death on the cross. He is aware that to those who see an absence of this joy on the faces of the Christians they meet, Christianity's claims ring hollow. However, he suggests that few people today actually know anything about Christianity, even though they think they do. 'There needs to be a renewal of what you could call a curiosity about Christianity; the desire really to discover what it's all about.'

He detects a growing disenchantment with secular culture and a spiritual hunger amongst many, particularly the young. 'To live without faith means then, to find oneself first in some sort of nihilistic state and then, nonetheless, to search for reference points,' he suggests. These reference points can be seen today not only in the supermarket of beliefs now on offer in the West, but also in the way football, health and fitness and celebrities become almost a quasi-religion to some.

Like Father Timothy Radcliffe, Benedict, too, talks of the

Church as 'pilgrim communities'. It was significant that the image on the gold vestments he wore at his installation Mass was a shell, a symbol of the Christian pilgrimage and one of the images he has had included on his coat of arms.

He has spoken of monasteries, once again, playing a key role in nurturing and sustaining the faith of Christians, in the same way they did in pagan times. To be a Christian, he says, means not to live in isolation but to be in communion with other 'wayfarers', committed Christians, to support each other along the journey of faith:

> Perhaps the time has come to say farewell to the idea
> of traditionally Catholic cultures. Maybe we are
> facing a new and different kind of epoch in the
> Church's history, where Christianity will again be
> characterized more by the mustard seed, where it will
> exist in small, seemingly insignificant groups that
> nonetheless live an intense struggle against evil and
> bring the good into the world.

While some churches count their effectiveness in terms of membership, Benedict firmly rejects this approach. Statistics, he says, are not an accurate indicator of the spiritual health of the Church, which is 'not a business operation that can look at the numbers to measure whether our policy has been successful and whether we're selling more and more.'

During the liturgies of the papal transition and election, Benedict gave a high profile to the Eastern-rite Catholic Church, numbering around 20 million members and scattered chiefly around Eastern Europe and the Middle East and sandwiched between Orthodoxy and Islam. The ancient chants of Eastern-rite patriarchs rose up over John Paul's simple coffin, while the gospel was sung in both Latin and Greek at his funeral Mass and Benedict's installation Mass. This could be read as a reminder of the Church's origins and also that it is not a Western institution.

New movements

At the heart of Pope Benedict's vision of a re-evangelization of Europe are the new movements, such as Communion and Liberation, Opus Dei, the Legionaries of Christ, and the Neo-Catechumenate. At Pentecost in 1998 an estimated 500,000 members of around 200 such communities arrived in Rome for a meeting called by Pope John Paul. In an address, the then Cardinal Ratzinger spoke about how, at different points in history, the Holy Spirit brings about dynamic movements, such as the monks inspired by Benedict, the friars in the Middle Ages, and the Jesuits after the Reformation to renew the Church.

He believes these new movements, which consist of lay people and priests, offer many, especially the young, the challenges they are seeking in life. With their stress on the sacraments, communal prayer, traditional devotions such as the rosary, and an enthusiasm to share the Christian message, the new movements are not only helping their members to live out their faith in a counter-cultural way, but also nurturing and producing urgently needed vocations to the priesthood and religious life.

In Vienna the Emmanuelle Community hold week-long 'city missions' in European capital cities. In northern Spain, Opus Dei runs the University of Navarre, which has 15,000 students, while former London gangster John Pridmore spearheads Youth 2000 missions in schools and parishes across Ireland. All of this leads Pope Benedict to say confidently that history 'is not in the hands of dark powers'.

Alongside them, new religious orders are springing up, such as The Monastic Family Fraternity of Jesus at Vallechiara, just south of Rome, which takes its inspiration partly from St Benedict and has a 70-strong youthful community drawn from across the world. The bearded Franciscan Friars of the Renewal have expanded from the streets of South Bronx in New York, where they work with the destitute and broken, to the East End of London.

Pope Benedict wants to see a renewal of the liturgy, which he talks of as 'heaven torn open here'. This sense of the sacred was lost, he believes, in the 'wild creativity' introduced by Vatican II. He says that, yes, the readings from the Bible should be in the vernacular but most of the other elements of the Mass should be in Latin. He points out that the reason the priest had his back to the people in the old Mass was positive, not negative, as some hold: it meant that the priest and people were facing God together, usually east, which was traditional, as the sun was seen to represent the Risen Christ.

What these new movements and religious orders do is help ordinary men and women who become 'lights for mankind' and start 'silent revolutions', in other words, saints, living their faith each day. Benedict says, 'What is important for me is to see the many inconspicuous saints, simple people like the ones I got to know in my childhood, the kind old farmers, kind dutiful mothers, who have given up their lives for their children, for the Church, and always for the other people in the village as well.'

The future

Bob Moynihan, editor of the magazine *Inside the Vatican*, says that Benedict exemplifies the paradox of Christianity by being both radical and conservative:

> He takes both positions to their extremes, therefore his mind is a broad mind which realizes that if you don't conserve things, you don't have any place to depart from; any thing to build on. In a way, it's called the democracy of the dead. If you don't respect what Athanasius, Augustine, Aquinas, Bellarmine and Newman said and did, then you are disrespectful to your own forbears and you are unfair to those who

follow after you if you don't provide them with a bridge from them to the future.

At the same time, you have to react to the changes of our times. No one could have ever imagined the changes that John Paul II brought in but at his right hand all this time was Ratzinger. They were always open in many ways to these changes and in modernizing the Church in a way that really upset the more traditional Catholics. In his homily at the end of the conclave he talked about peace and reconciliation and he's indicated an openness to the Orthodox and the Protestants and two other faiths. I think we are in for a wild ride.

Pope Benedict's vision of the Church in the twenty-first century, then, is of small, dynamic communities, similar to the monasteries that sprang up across Europe as a result of St Benedict's Rule. These communities are not to become exclusive – nor are they to replace parishes – but must reach out to all, he stresses.

The Church of the first three centuries was a small Church and nevertheless was not a sectarian community. On the contrary, she was not partitioned off; rather, she saw herself as responsible for the poor, for the sick, for everyone. All those who sought a faith in one God, who sought a promise, found their place in her.

I have nothing against it, then, if people who all year long never visit a church go there at last on Christmas night or New Year's Eve or on special occasions, because this is another way of belonging to the blessing of the sacred, to the light. There have to be various forms of participation and association; the Church must be inwardly open.

Pope John XXIII was seen as a caretaker pontiff because of his age, and there are those who may be tempted to view 78-year-old Pope Benedict XVI in a similar way, or to see him as simply an imitation of John Paul II. This would be a mistake. For the Church is now being led by a man who might turn out to be one of the most radical and inspiring popes ever. We have entered the New Benedictine Age.

Bibliography

John L. Allen, Jr., *Cardinal Ratzinger: The Vatican's Enforcer of the Faith*, Continuum, 2002.

John L. Allen, Jr., *Conclave: The Politics, Personalities, and Process of the Next Papal Election*, Doubleday, 2002.

John L. Allen, Jr., *All the Pope's Men: The Inside Story of How the Vatican Really Thinks*, Doubleday, 2004.

John Cornwell, *Breaking Faith: The Pope, the People and the Fate of Catholicism*, Viking, 2001.

Adrian Hastings (ed.), *Modern Catholicism: Vatican II and After*, SPCK, 1991.

Peter Hebblethwaite, *The Runaway Church*, Fount, 1978.

Jonathan Kwitny, *Man of the Century: The Life and Times of Pope John Paul II*, Little Brown, 1997.

Joseph Cardinal Ratzinger, *Milestones, Memoirs 1927–1977*, Ignatius Press, 1998.

Joseph Cardinal Ratzinger, *God and the World: Believing and Living in Our Time, A Conversation with Peter Seewald*, translated by Henry Taylor, Ignatius Press, 2000.

Joseph Cardinal Ratzinger, *Many Religions – One Covenant: Israel, the Church and the World*, Ignatius Press, 1998.

Joseph Cardinal Ratzinger, *Gospel, Catechesis, Catechism: Sidelights on the Catechism of the Catholic Church*, Ignatius Press, 1995.

Joseph Cardinal Ratzinger, *Salt of the Earth: The Church at the End of the Millennium. An Interview with Peter Seewald*, Ignatius Press, 1997.

Joseph Cardinal Ratzinger with Vittorio Messori, *The Ratzinger Report: An Exclusive Interview on the State of the Catholic Church*, Ignatius Press, 1985.

David Rice, *Shattered Vows: Exodus From the Priesthood*, Michael Joseph, 1990.

George Weigel, *Witness to Hope; The Biography of Pope John Paul II*, HarperCollins, 1999.

George Weigel, *The Courage to be Catholic: Crisis, Reform and the Future of the Church*, Basic Books, 2002.

Other resources

www.indcatholicnews.com   Independent Catholic News
www.ratzingerfanclub.com   The Cardinal Ratzinger Fan Club
www.vatican.va   The official Vatican website
www.zenit.org   Zenit, International News Agency

Acknowledgments

I am grateful to all those who gave me their stories or insights about Pope Benedict XVI. Special thanks, however, must go to veteran journalist Peter Jennings, who not only shared his terrific knowledge of Rome and the Church with me, but also provided an unforgettable moment one afternoon when he pursued an astonished and alarmed Cardinal Francis Arinze across St Peter's Square. I'd also like to thank everyone at the Catholic Communications Network and the staff and students at the Venerable English College, particularly Bruno Witchalls. Other thanks go to Saxon Bashford, Father Ben Kiely, Father Tony Ward, David Armstrong, Sister Janet Fearns at Vatican Radio, Jo Siedlecka of Independent Catholic News and Abbot Cuthbert Johnson of Quarr Abbey. I must not forget Archbishop Vincent Nichols of Birmingham whose unintentional appearance on the podium in the Paul VI Hall alongside Pope Benedict XVI, at his meeting with the world's media, is another memory I will cherish from that extraordinary time in Rome in April 2005. Finally, I would like to thank Morag Reeve at Lion Hudson for commissioning me to write this book and Su Box for copy-editing it.

Picture acknowledgments

Page 1 of 4: Getty Images (above and below right); STF/AFP/Getty Images (below left).
Page 2 of 4: AP/EMPICS (above); Bettmann/Corbis (below).
Page 3 of 4: Patrick Hertzog/AFP/Getty Images (above and below).
Page 4 of 4: Filippo Monteforte/AFP/Getty Images (above left); Getty Images (above right); Fotografia Felici (below).

All Lion Books are available from your local bookshop, or can be ordered via our website or from Marston Book Services. For a free catalogue, showing the complete list of titles available, please contact:

Customer Services
Marston Book Services
PO Box 269
Abingdon
Oxon
OX14 4YN

Tel: 01235 465500
Fax: 01235 465555

Our website can be found at:
www.lionhudson.com